VIA VERTENDI

VIA VERTENDI

A LATIN UNSEEN COURSE

B.W.M. YOUNG

Bristol Classical Press

First published in 1952 by Longmans Green and Co. Ltd

This edition published in 1992,
by arrangement with Longman Group UK, by
Bristol Classical Press
an imprint of
Gerald Duckworth & Co. Ltd
61 Frith Street
London W1D 3JL
e-mail: inquiries@duckworth-publishers.co.uk

Reprinted 1996, 2001

A catalogue record for this book is available
from the British Library

ISBN 1-85399-327-1

Printed in Great Britain by
Antony Rowe Ltd, Eastbourne

PREFACE

— But you must know 'tamen'?

— Never seen it in my life.

— And surely the story meant something to you?

— Oh, sir! I thought this was just an unseen.

This kind of conversation, which is not unknown to school-teachers, came to mind when it was suggested to me that a new Unseen Book was needed; and in the hope of making such exchanges less common I have added some features to the normal collection of unseens.

Plenty of Latin courses hammer home points about translating English into Latin; but sporadic work at unseens often produces the same mistake every other week, as 'ut' with the indicative or 'qui' at the beginning of a sentence is mistranslated with dreary regularity. This book is intended therefore to be a course and to give systematic help with Latin–English translation. There are obvious difficulties: one is that the instruction given must be simple and light in tone, if the book is not to become a grammar with exercises, and yet it must cover the ground; another is that constructions cannot be kept out of unseens until the time comes for them to be discussed. It is assumed therefore that Latin is not here absolutely new to the pupils; but each chapter deals with some important facts, including several they should know already, from a translator's view-point, and the three following unseens drive home points brought out in the chapter as fully as possible: cross-references from an unseen to another part of the book are quite freely given to help with difficulties, but they need not of course be used. Even if nothing else is achieved by this system, we shall at least be able to show pupils where they learnt (or should have learnt) a common point and to find out if they are making progress.

In the second place, the book is intended to present the unseens not as mere slabs of Latin, having no connection with anything else, but as living and interesting pieces of writing which are more than just 'tests'. With this in view I have used stories as the basis of the easy 'A' pieces (which could well be done orally at the beginning of a period); and for the 'B' and 'C' unseens I have chosen (and sometimes adapted) worthwhile pieces from a variety of authors, as far as this was possible. The notes at the end of the book are, of necessity, short and offer hints that a teacher can amplify: apart from giving some information about the writers and about the Greek and Roman background, they are meant to connect the unseens with other reading (mainly English) and to provoke thought.

The help provided in the unseens consists of footnotes and (in the 'A' pieces) the marking of long syllables where the quantity is relevant. In the footnotes I have sometimes preferred pointing the way to giving the answer outright; this takes longer but may show a pupil how to tackle difficulties when no help is given.

My debt to the standard works of reference is obvious; and those who have given me more direct help (the elder by their criticisms and the younger by the mistakes they made) would for different reasons prefer to remain anonymous. I record my gratitude to them, but name no names.

B.W.M.Y.

vi

CONTENTS

PART I

vii

PART II

PART I

PROLOGUE

An Unseen must first be understood, then translated.

1. Understand.

Until you are practised in reading Latin, you must *analyse* in order to *understand*. You are therefore shown how to find the ' bones ' of a sentence— subject, verb, and object or complement. Once you have found these, you can fit in adjectives, adverbs, prepositional phrases, etc.

Subordinate clauses must be recognized and dealt with separately: they, like the main sentence, have their ' bones ' and follow the same rules, with allowance for special circumstances, *e.g.* for the fact that ' qui ' may be the subject—or ' quem ' the object—of its clause.

In all this you will be helped by a knowledge of English grammar and of the structure of a sentence.

Some people, while in the process of understanding an unseen, bracket off subordinate clauses and under- line words that they do not know in order to return and guess them later (*see* Chapter XV). This may be useful, but it is better to do these things in your head—and it makes the book last longer.

2. **Translate.**

When you have understood the meaning of a piece, you must *translate it into good English:* at least half the value of an unseen lies in the practice it gives you in handling your own language. There is no need to add the literal meaning of the Latin in brackets to your English translation : a good rendering will show that you have understood the original —but you should not change the Latin construction when you need not (for that would suggest inaccuracy and guessing).

Two words of warning:—

(i) *Do not write as if each Latin word had only one English equivalent.* ' Res,' for example, has a dozen, and you must choose the one that fits the context.

(ii) *Do not suppose, when you meet a proper name, that all the work is done for you.* Even though a word begins with a capital letter, it may well be in an oblique case : in your rendering, its nominative (and, if necessary, its English form) must appear. Note that we usually translate *Poeni* as *Carthaginians,* and *Lacedaemonii* as *Spartans.*

WHICH IS THE MAIN VERB?

1. *Know what you are looking for.* Participles and gerunds should be ignored in this first search. For the main verb will be usually in the INDICATIVE, occasionally in the *imperative* or *subjunctive*, and very occasionally in the infinitive.

2. *Bracket off subordinate clauses in your mind.* Words like ' qui,' ' cum,' ' ut,' ' si,' and ' quamquam,' will be followed by the verbs of their own clauses. Ignore these for the present.

3. *Do one sentence at a time.* There may be further main verbs (introduced by ' et,' ' -que,' ' nec,' ' sed,' ' nam '—or even by no conjunction at all) : these do not concern you until you have made out the first sentence.

EXAMPLE :

' Imperator, quem haec res non terruerat, suos hortatus ut fortiter dimicarent, signa in hostes intulit, et proelium commisit.'

[When you have bracketed off ' quem . . . terruerat ' and ' suos . . . dimicarent,' the bones of the sentence remain. ' Intulit ' is the main verb : ' commisit ' is the main verb of a second sentence introduced by ' et.']

' The general, whom this occurrence had not

frightened, after encouraging his men to fight bravely, advanced against the enemy and joined battle.'

[*Note*.—Neither the first nor the last indicative of the sentence was the main verb you were first seeking. You must analyse the sentence carefully like this, until you are practised enough to do it instinctively.]

Note 1. *The tense of the main verb.*

You will usually have the same tense in English as in Latin.

But

(*a*) *In narrative pieces* Latin writers often use the *present*, where in English we use the *aorist*.

(*b*) With ' *iam dudum*,' ' *iam pridem* ' and ' *iam diu* ' (= ' for a long time '):—

the Latin *present* is translated by the English *perfect*:

the Latin *imperfect* is translated by the English *pluperfect*.

EXAMPLE :

' Iam pridem aegroto.'
' I have long been ill.'

Note 2. *The omission of the main verb.*

The main verb is sometimes omitted :

(*a*) When it can easily be supplied from the *previous or following sentence*.

(*b*) When it is a *part of* ' *sum*.' (This is especially common with *past participles*.)

EXAMPLE :

' Multi fugientes interfecti.'
' Many were killed while fleeing.'

4

Horatius kills his unpatriotic sister.

Horatius, postquam tres Curiatios interfecit, Romam redibat, trium hostium spolia in umeris[1] ferens, et laudes victori debitas[2] ab omnibus accipiebat. Sed soror eius, quae desponsa[3] uni ex Curiatiis fuerat, ante portam Capenam eum vidit; tum, veste sponsi, quam ipsa fecerat, super umeros fratris agnitā[4], solvit crines[5] et flens sponsum mortuum nomine appellavit. Movent Horatii iram lacrimae sororis inter tantum gaudium profusae: stricto igitur gladio puellam transfigit, quia patriam non satis amabat.

[1] ' *Shoulders.* '
[2] ' *Debeo* ' = ' *I owe* '; *therefore* ' *debitus* ' = ' *due.* '
[3] ' *Betrothed.* '
[4] ' *Agnosco* ' = ' *I recognize.* '
[5] ' *Crines* ' (*plural*) = ' *hair.* '

A brave standard-bearer leads the way from Caesar's fleet to the shores of Britain.

Nostris militibus cunctantibus[1], maxime propter altitudinem maris, is qui decimae legionis aquilam ferebat, contestatus[2] deos ut ea res legioni feliciter eveniret, ' Desilite,' inquit, ' milites, nisi vultis aquilam hostibus prodere : ego certe meum rei publicae atque imperatori officium praestitero.' Hoc cum voce magna dixisset, se ex navi proiecit atque in hostes aquilam ferre coepit. Tum nostri, cohortati inter se[3] ne tantum dedecus admitteretur, universi ex navi desiluerunt : hos cum alii ex proximis navibus conspexissent, subsecuti hostibus appropinquaverunt.

[1] ' *Cunctor* ' = ' *I delay.* '
[2] ' *Contestor* ' = ' *I call to witness.* '
[3] *See XXI. 3.*

A picture of the Golden Age, when life was easy and there was no travelling or warfare.

Quam bene Saturno vivebant rege, priusquam
    Tellus in longas est patefacta vias!
Nondum caeruleas pinus contempserat undas,
    Effusum ventis praebueratque[1] sinum[2] ;
Nec vagus, ignotis repetens compendia[3] terris,
    Presserat[4] externa navita merce ratem.
Illo non validus subiit iuga tempore taurus ;
    Non domito frenos[5] ore momordit equus ;
Non domus ulla fores habuit ; non fixus in agris,
    Qui regeret certis finibus arva, lapis.
Ipsae mella dabant quercus, ultroque ferebant
    Obvia securis ubera lactis oves.
Non acies, non ira fuit, non bella ; nec ensem
    Immiti saevus duxerat arte faber.

[1] *Occasionally, as here, ' -que,' though placed late, must be taken at the beginning of the line.*
[2] *' Sail.' The pine here stands for the ship made from its wood.*
[3] *' Gain.'*
[4] *' Premo '* = *' load ' (here).*
[5] *' Frenos '* = *' bit.' How will you translate ' momordit ' now?*

II

FIND THE SUBJECT

1. *The verb will tell you the person and number of the subject.*

EXAMPLES :

    (i) ' Studium in Caesarem milites habebant.'

        [' Habebant ' shows you that ' milites ' is the subject.]

      ' The soldiers were devoted to Caesar.'

    (ii) ' Tu, dea, tu praesens nostro succurre labori.'

        [The imperative ' succurre ' points to ' tu ' as subject and puts you on the look-out for a vocative—' dea.']

      ' Do thou, O goddess, help my efforts with timely aid.'

2. *If the subject is expressed*, it will usually be a *noun* or *pronoun* (as in the examples above). But it may be an *infinitive*.

EXAMPLE :

    ' Dulce est desipere in loco.'

    ' To play the fool in season is pleasant.'

[Or we may translate : ' It is pleasant to . . .]

3. *If the subject is not expressed,* it may be
    (*a*) In the verb.

EXAMPLE :

    ' Oderint, dum metuant.'

    ' Let them hate, provided that they fear.'

(*b*) Understood, with an *adjective, participle* or *relative clause*.

EXAMPLES :

> (i) ' Sapientes adfirmant . . .'
> ' Wise *men* declare . . .'
>
> (ii) ' Qui hanc rem intelligunt, adfirmant . . .'
> ' *Those* who understand this question declare . . .'

Note 1. *Impersonal Constructions* (with ' *it* ' as subject in the verb) are dealt with in chapter XIII.

Note 2. *A double subject* may be followed by either a *singular* or a *plural* verb.

EXAMPLE :

' Haec arma et Aiax et Ulixes $\begin{cases} \text{cupiebat.'} \\ \text{cupiebant.'} \end{cases}$

' Both Ajax and Ulysses longed for this armour.'

An old man teaches his sons that unity is strength.

Senex, cuius filii perpetuas inter se rixas[1] habebant, diu pacare[2] eos frustra conabatur : tandem eos exemplo docere constituit. Septem igitur virgis[3], quas de arboribus carpserat, fascem[4] fecit et hunc natu maximo traditum frangi iussit. Summa vi nitebatur et hic et fratres ut fascem frangerent, nec tamen quicquam efficiebant. Tum unam de virgis raptam pater filiis porrexit[5] : et hanc et sex alias de fasce ademptas[6] facile fregerunt ei, quibus eaedem colligatae[7] tam validae esse videbantur. Itaque pater 'Nonne videtis, filii,' inquit, 'quam utile sit coniungi ? Nam facile superatur qui solus manet : sed qui cum suis consociatur nunquam hostes timet.'

[1] ' *Quarrels.*'
[2] ' *Reconcile.*'
[3] ' *Virga* ' = ' *twig.*'
[4] ' *Fascis* ' = ' *bundle.*'
[5] ' *Porrigo* ' = ' *I hold out.*'
[6] ' *Adimo* ' = ' *I take away.*'
[7] *From* ' *con-ligare.*' *Guess the meaning from the context if you do not know* ' *ligare* ' (*or the English* ' *ligament* ' *or* ' *ligature* ').

Caesar's arrival brings victory.

Labienus, postquam neque aggeres neque fossae vim hostium sustinere poterant, Caesarem per nuntios facit certiorem quid faciendum[1] existimet. Accelerat Caesar ut proelio intersit[2]. Eius adventu ex colore vestitus cognito, hostes proelium committunt. Utrimque clamore sublato, excipit[3] rursus ex vallo atque omnibus munitionibus clamor. Nostri omissis pilis, gladiis rem gerunt. Repente post tergum[4] equitatus cernitur: cohortes aliae appropinquant. Hostes terga vertunt; fugientibus equites occurrunt[5]: fit magna caedes: pauci ex tanto numero se incolumes in castra recipiunt.

[1] *See XII. 1. ((b).*
[2] *' Take part in.'*
[3] *' Follows ' (intr.).*
[4] *Whose back is referred to ?   Your common sense and the rest of the piece will tell you.*
[5] *' Occurro ' + dative = ' I meet.'*

Aeneas describes the Trojans' first view of Italy.

Iamque rubescebat stellis Aurora fugatis,
Cum procul obscuros colles humilemque videmus
Italiam. ' Italiam ' primus conclamat Achates,
Italiam laeto socii clamore salutant.
Tum pater Anchises magnum cratera[1] corona
Induit implevitque mero divosque vocavit,
Stans celsa in puppi :
' Di maris et terrae tempestatumque potentes,
Ferte[2] viam vento facilem et spirate secundi !'
Crebrescunt[3] optatae aurae, portusque patescit
Iam propior, templumque apparet in arce Minervae.

[1] *Accusative singular of ' crater ' = ' bowl.' To wreathe a bowl
was a solemn act in calling on the gods.*

[2] *When you have decided what each word means, think what
Anchises wanted—a fair passage to the shore—and translate
accordingly.*

[3] *' Creber ' (= ' frequent ') may help here.*

III

AN OBJECT OR TWO

1. *Is there an object at all?*

If the verb is *intransitive* or *passive*, you will not go on to look for a direct object. But, if there is an object, the verb will suggest the sort of word you want. [*E.g.* in 3 (*c*) example, below, ' aedificare ' points to ' murum.']

2. *Will the object be in the accusative?*

Yes: unless the verb is one which takes the genitive, dative, or ablative (*see* chapters VII–IX)—in which case you have in the verb a warning.

3. *What else may be in the accusative case?*

(*a*) *Prepositions* may claim some accusatives: bracket these phrases off in your mind at first.

(*b*) An ' *accusative and infinitive* ' construction may introduce accusatives which are not the object: but the verb will have warned you to expect this.

(*c*) Some expressions of *direction, extent,* and *time,* employ the accusative.

EXAMPLE:

' Tres dies murum decem pedes altum aedificare
    conabatur.'
' For three days he was trying to build a wall
    ten feet high.'

4. *Is there a second object?*

(*a*) Verbs of *giving, promising, showing, telling,* and *taking away,* and many *verbs compounded with prepositions,* often take an INDIRECT OBJECT IN THE DATIVE as well as a DIRECT OBJECT IN THE ACCUSATIVE. This second object completes the sense of the verb, and is not difficult to see, once the meaning of the verb has been grasped.

EXAMPLES :

    (i) ' Lyciis libertatem ademit, Rhodiis reddidit.'
       ' He took from the Lycians their freedom,
        but gave back to the Rhodians theirs.'

    (ii) ' Te classi praeficio.'
      ' I put you in command of the fleet.'

(*b*) A few verbs, like *doceo* and *rogo* can have TWO OBJECTS IN THE ACCUSATIVE, one of the person and one of the thing.

EXAMPLE :

    ' Quid nunc te, asine, litteras doceam ? '
    ' Why should I now teach you letters, you ass ? '

[*Note.*—This construction should not be confused with that of OBJECT and PREDICATE, IV. 2. (*b*)].

Polycrates tries to escape the gods' jealousy of his good fortune.

Inter Graecos multi credebant deos nemini res secundas[1] per totam vitam tribuere. Polycrates igitur, qui tyrannus felicissimus erat, hoc consilium cepit ne, fortunā nimium[2] sublatus, invidiam[3] deorum moveret: anulum[4] quem pulcherrimum in thesauro[5] suo habebat de nave in mare iecit. Domum regressus quinque dies dolebat quod hunc tam carum anulum amiserat. Sexto die quidam e civibus piscem tam grandem cepit ut eum tyranno dare constituerit. Cum tamen servi piscem ad prandium secuissent, anulum eundem intus inventum[6] summo cum gaudio Polycrati reddiderunt. Sic tyrannus bonā fortunā uti[7] non desinebat[8]; sed mox dei calamitatem multo maiorem ei intulerunt.

[1] ' Secundus ' = ' favourable ' : ' res secundae ' can be translated by one English noun.

[2] ' Too much.'

[3] Guess this word from the heading and from an English word that is like it.

[4] ' Ring.'

[5] ' Treasure-chamber.'

[6] See XI. 2. (a).

[7] ' Utor ' serves in many Latin phrases and must not always be translated as ' use.'

[8] ' Desino ' = ' cease.'

Two light-hearted robberies.

Dionysius, cum fanum Proserpinae Locris ex-
pilavisset[1], navigabat Syracusas : isque, cum secun-
dissimo vento cursum teneret, ridens, ' Videtisne,'
inquit, ' amici, quam bona a dis immortalibus
navigatio sacrilegis detur ? ' Idem, cum ad Pelo-
ponnesum classem appulisset, et in fanum venisset
Iovis Olympii, aureum ei detraxit amiculum[2], quo
Iovem ornaverat ex manubiis[3] Carthaginiensium
tyrannus Hiero. Atque in eo etiam cavillatus[4] est,
aestate grave esse aureum amiculum, hieme frigidum,
eique laneum palleum[2] iniecit, cum id esse aptum
ad omne anni tempus diceret.

[1] ' Had plundered.' ' Locris ' is the locative of ' Locri.'
[2] ' Cloak.'
[3] ' Spoils.'
[4] ' Cavillor ' = ' I make a joke.' As it is followed by the
accusative and infinitive, you will probably put in the words ' saying
that . . .' in your translation.

The fame of Arion, who charmed all with his music.

Quod mare non novit, quae nescit Ariona tellus?
  Carmine currentes ille tenebat aquas.
Saepe, sequens agnam, lupus est a voce retentus,
  Saepe avidum fugiens restitit[1] agna lupum:
Saepe canes leporesque umbra cubuere sub una,
  Et stetit in saxo proxima cerva leae[2]:
Et sine lite loquax cum Palladis alite[3] cornix
  Sedit, et accipitri[4] iuncta columba fuit.
Cynthia saepe tuis fertur, vocalis Arion,
  Tamquam fraternis[5] obstupuisse modis.
Nomen Arionium Siculas impleverat urbes,
  Captaque erat lyricis Ausonis ora sonis.

[1] ' *Restitit* ' *is intransitive.*
[2] ' *Lea* ' = ' *lioness.*'
[3] *Pallas' bird was the owl.*
[4] ' *Hawk.*'
[5] *Apollo, god of music, was the brother of Cynthia (Diana).*

APPOSITION AND COMPLEMENT

1. Apposition.

(*a*) A second noun in the nominative is often added to the subject to tell you more about it ; this second noun is said to be *in apposition*.

EXAMPLE :

' Coleus, rex Angliae, saepe gavisus est.'

' Cole, King of England, often rejoiced.'

[The commas always show which noun is subject, and it is a silly mistake to translate the above sentence as—

' The King of England, Cole, often rejoiced.']

(*b*) Sometimes a word is in apposition to a subject ' in the verb.'

EXAMPLE :

' Ad te supplex venio.'

' I come to you as a suppliant.'

(*c*) Nouns in apposition may be added to nouns and pronouns in any case : they always agree with the word to which they refer.

EXAMPLE :

' Tibi puero adversatus sum.'

' I opposed you when you were a boy.'

(Literally, ' . . . you as a boy.')

2. Complement.

(*a*) The verbs *sum* and *fio*, and a few others, of which the commonest are *videor* (I seem), *creor* (I

am appointed), and *habeor* (I am considered), are
followed by a *complement*.   Such a verb will warn
you that there may be two words in the nominative
case : and common sense (and often the order) will
tell you which is subject, and which complement.

EXAMPLES :

    (i) ' Hi consules facti sunt.'
       ' These men were made consuls.'

   (ii) ' Et rex et pater omnium habetur.'
       ' He is considered both king and father of
         all men.'

(*b*) Similarly, the *actives* of these verbs will often
be followed by *two accusatives,* one the object and
one the predicate.

EXAMPLE :

   ' Heredem filiam fecit.'
   ' He appointed his daughter as his heir.'

A boy's brave reply.

Hannibal, imperator fortissimus, dum bellum in Italiā gerit, multos captivos Romanos quondam cepit; inter eos puer erat, quattuordecim annos natus, quēm omnes tĭmidum habebant. Sed idem, cum Hannibal interrogavisset quis esset, nihil territus, ' Romanus sum,' respondit: ' pater meus senator est.' Tum Hannibal, ' Nonne vis,' rogavit, ' Carthagiensis fieri et me sequi ? ' Puer tamen, ' Malo,' respondit, ' Romanus honestē mori quam Carthaginiensis turpiter vivere.' Hannibal igitur, virtutem eius admiratus, ' Si tibi puero,' inquit, ' tantus est amor patriae, qualis vir eris! ' Et puerum domum misit incolumem.[1]

[1] *See V. 2. (a).*

A haunted house.

Erat Athenis spatiosa et capax domus, sed infamis et pestilens. Per silentium noctis sonus ferri et strepitus vinculorum longius primo, deinde e proximo reddebatur[1] : mox apparebat idolon[2], senex macie et squalore confectus, promissa barba[3], horrenti capillo ; cruribus compedes, manibus catenas[4] gerebat quatiebatque. Inde inhabitantibus[5] tristes diraeque noctes per metum vigilabantur[6] : vigiliam[6] morbus et, crescente formidine, mors sequebatur. Nam interdiu quoque quamquam abscesserat imago, memoria imaginis oculis inerrabat, longiorque causis timoris timor erat.

[1] Lit. ' give forth ' : translate ' used to be heard.'

[2] Nominative : = ghost.

[3] See IX. 1. (vi).

[4] ' Chains.'

[5] This is dative but you will probably turn the sentence so that in English it is the subject.

[6] What do the English words ' vigil ' and ' vigilant ' mean ?

Cornelia addresses her husband from the grave, bidding him care for their children and hide his grief for her from them.

Nunc tibi commendo, communia pignora, natos;
    Haec cura et cineri spirat inusta[1] meo.
Fungere maternis vicibus, pater.   Illa meorum
    Omnis erit collo[2] turba ferenda tuo.
Oscula cum dederis tua flentibus, adice[3] matris:
    Tota domus coepit nunc onus esse tuum.
Et si quid doliturus eris, sine testibus illis[4];
    Cum venient, siccis oscula[5] falle genis.
Sat tibi sint noctes, quas de me, Paulle, fatiges,
    Somniaque in faciem credita saepe meam.

    [1] *From ' uro ' = ' I burn.'*
    [2] *On what part of the body do you wear a collar ?*
    [3] *A compound of ' iacio.'*
    [4] *Understand ' dolē ' here.*
    [5] *Lit. = ' kisses,' here = ' them as they kiss you.'*

V

FIT THE ADJECTIVE

1. *Fit each adjective to the noun with which it agrees in number, gender and case.*

Obvious enough: but carelessness is responsible for many mistakes here—adjectives attached to the wrong nouns, adverbs treated as adjectives, and so on. In verse the noun is frequently separated from its adjective (note that, if they follow a preposition, it can go with either); but, if you know ' bonus ' and ' tristis ' and use your common sense, you cannot go wrong.

EXAMPLE:

' Prima malas docuit, mirantibus aequoris undis

Peliaco pinus vertice caesa vias.'

' The pine that was cut on the summit of Pelion was the first to teach accursed voyaging, while the waves of the sea looked on in amazement.'

2. *An adjective in Latin is not always to be translated by an English adjective.*

(a) Sometimes, especially when it agrees with a subject that is ' in the verb ', it should be rendered by an adverb.

23

> ' Invitus ad bellum profectus est, sed incolumis
>   rediit.'

> ' He set off to the war unwillingly, but returned
>   safely ' (*or* ' in safety').

(*b*) Sometimes, especially with *medius, summus, imus* and *reliquus*, the English equivalent is ' the . . . of . . .'

EXAMPLE :

> ' Reliqui cives ad imum montem ierunt.'

> ' The rest of the citizens went to the bottom
>   of the mountain.'

3. *A relative clause does the work of an adjective.* It also must be correctly fitted to the noun which it concerns (the ' antecedent ') : again gender and number will help and the order is almost always important.

> *Note :* Participles also do the work of adjectives,
> but these deserve a chapter to themselves (XI).

Perverse pigs.

Dum laetus ad summum collem ambulo, subito agricolae, qui sues pingues agebat, occurri[1]. Tum ego, ' Salvē!' inquam : ' quo hos sues agis ? ' Ille respondit se Thebas ire. At ego, incredibilem stultitiam hominis miratus, clamavi, ' Haec via ad Thebas non fert, sed ad Plataeas.' Tum agricola, verbis meis turbatus, ' St! tacē! ' inquit. ' Plataeas re verā eo, sed simulo[2] me urbem alteram petere ; nam hi sues tam obstinati sunt ut, quamvis magno cum labore acti, nolint ire quo velim ; nunc tamen, rati[3] me Thebas petere, prompti Plataeas currunt.'

[1] See 2 B.
[2] ' I pretend.'
[3] ' Ratus ' is the perfect participle of ' reor.'

5 B

A description of the Caudine Forks.

Duae ad Luceriam ferebant viae; altera praeter
oram superi maris patens apertaque, sed, quanto
tutior, tanto fere longior; altera per Furculas
Caudinas, brevior.   Sed ita natus[1] locus est: saltus
duo alti angusti silvosique sunt, montibus circa perpetuis inter se iuncti: iacet inter eos satis patens
clausus in medio campus, herbidus aquosusque, per
quem medium iter est.   Sed, antequam venias ad
eum, intrandae[2] primae angustiae sunt: et aut
eadem, qua te insinuaveris, retro via repetenda[2];
aut, si ire porro pergas, per alium saltum artiorem
impeditioremque evadendum[2].

[1] *Not here ' born,' but ' formed.'*
[2] *See XII. 1. (b).*

*Notice throughout this piece that the main verb is sometimes
omitted in Latin, but you must supply it in English.*

The poet wishes in vain for a means of revisiting his home.

Nunc ego Triptolemi[1] cuperem conscendere currus,
  Misit in ignotam qui rude semen humum :
Nunc ego Medeae vellem frenare dracones,
  Quos habuit fugiens arce, Corinthe, tua :
Nunc ego iactandas optarem sumere pennas
  Sive tuas, Perseu, Daedale, sive tuas ;
Ut, tenera nostris cedente[2] volatibus aura,
  Aspicerem patriae dulce repente solum,
Desertaeque domus vultum, memoresque sodales,
  Caraque praecipue coniugis ora meae.
Stulte, quid[3] o frustra votis puerilibus optas,
  Quae non ulla tibi fertque feretque dies ?

[1] *Triptolemus was sent flying over the earth by Demeter to teach men the art of agriculture.*
[2] ' *Cedo* ' = ' *yield,*' ' *give way to.*'
[3] *See XXIII. 1. Note 2.*

WHY SUBJUNCTIVE ?

When you have discovered the main verb, you may find that it is in the subjunctive : do not ignore this as a curious accident, but ask yourself WHY.

1. The commonest reason is that it expresses a *command* (or, with the negative ' *ne*,' a *prohibition*).

EXAMPLES :

    (i) ' Properemus ' = ' Let us hasten.'
    (ii) ' Ne conentur ' = ' Let them not try.'
    (iii) ' Ne rogaveris ' = ' Do not ask.'

2. In a question the subjunctive may well be *deliberative*, *i.e.* it suggests the hesitation and thought of the person answering the question.

EXAMPLE :

    ' Quid faceret ? quo se raptā bis coniuge ferret ?'
    ' What was he to do ?   Whither should he go, now that his wife had twice been taken from him ?'

3. In a *conditional sentence* which denotes a remote possibility, the main verb is usually in the same subjunctive as the verb in the ' *si* ' *clause*.

EXAMPLE :

    ' Si eum moneas, desinat canere.'
    ' If you warned him, he would stop singing.'
Sometimes the ' si ' clause is omitted or understood :

(i) ' Credas eum insanum esse.'

' You would think him mad ' (if you saw him).

(ii) ' A te monitus, canere desinat.'

'(If) warned by you, he would stop singing.'

4. *Wishes*, often (but not always) introduced by ' *utinam* ' or ' *o si*,' take the subjunctive : the tenses are the same as in Conditional Sentences.

EXAMPLE :

' Utinam populus Romanus unam cervicem haberet! '

' Would that the Roman people had only one neck! '

5. A sentence denoting *possibility* (usually with *forsitan* or *forsan*) may cause the main verb to be in the subjunctive.

EXAMPLE :

' Forsitan quaeratis . . .'

' Perhaps you may ask . . .'

Note 1. There are several key-words (*e.g.* ' *ne* ', ' *si* ', and ' *forsitan* ') in these constructions : with the help of these—and the ? in 2, and the ! in 4— you should be able to see why any main verb is in the subjunctive.

Note 2. You should also always satisfy yourself that you know the reason, when a verb *in a subordinate clause* is in the subjunctive : but, as it would take several pages to list the constructions here, you must learn them elsewhere.

A murder is revealed by dreams.

Cum duo amici, qui iter unā faciebant, Megaram
venissent, alter ad cauponem[1], alter ad hospitem
devertit[2]. Dum hic dormit, ille apparere in somnis
visus, ' Utinam tu mecum esses! ' inquit. ' Nam
cauponi in animo est me occidere. Sed tu ne
cessaveris[3], sed statim fer mihi auxilium : tum ambo
e periculis huius oppidi effugiamus.' ' Quid faciam ?'
clamavit alter, perterritus, sed, simul atque se
somniare[4] percepit, gavisus quod timor inanis[5] videbatur, iterum dormivit. At imago[5] amici, oculis
huius iterum oblata, ' Eheu! ' inquit : ' propter
inertiam[5] tuam occisus sum. Sed ne evadat[5]
caupo. Plaustro[6] eius prope portam māne[7] ex-
cepto, cadaver[5] meum intus invenies.' Hōc somnio
commotus, surrexit et plaustrum mane scrutatus est ;
cadavere invento, caupo poenas dedit.

[1] ' Caupo ' = ' innkeeper ' (contrasted with ' hospes ').
[2] ' Deverto ' lit. = ' I turn aside,' and hence ' I stay the night.'
[3] ' Cesso ' = ' I delay.'
[4] ' Somnio ' = ' I dream.'
[5] All these words can be guessed, if you do not know them, either
from English words like them or from the context.
[6] ' Plaustrum ' = ' waggon.'
[7] ' Mane ' = ' in the morning.'

L. Aemilius Paullus, the consul, refuses a tribune's offer to save him after the battle of Cannae.

Cn. Lentulus tribunus militum cum praeter-vehens[1] equo sedentem in saxo cruore oppletum[2] consulem vidisset, ' L. Aemili,' inquit, ' quem unum insontem culpae cladis hodiernae dei respicere debent, cape hunc equum, dum et tibi virium aliquid superest, et comes ego te tollere possum ac protegere. Ne funestam hanc pugnam morte consulis feceris ; etiam sine hoc lacrimarum satis luctusque est.' Ad ea consul : ' Tu quidem, Cn. Corneli, macte[3] virtute esto ; sed cave ne frustra miserando exiguum tempus e manibus hostium evadendi absumas. Abi, nuntia publice patribus, urbem Romanam muniant ac, priusquam victor hostis adveniat, praesidiis firment ; privatim Q. Fabio L. Aemilium praeceptorum eius memorem et vixisse adhuc et mori.'

[1] *This is the participle of ' praetervehor ' = ' I ride past.'*

[2] *' Covered.'*

[3] *If you do not know this phrase, think what the consul would naturally say at this moment.*

The poet speaks of his death to Delia, his love.

Te spectem, suprema mihi cum venerit hora,
  Et teneam moriens deficiente manu.
Flebis et arsuro positum me, Delia, lecto[1],
  Tristibus et lacrimis oscula mixta dabis.
Flebis: non tua sunt duro praecordia ferro
  Vincta, nec in tenero stat tibi corde silex.
Illo non iuvenis poterit de funere quisquam
  Lumina[2], non virgo sicca referre domum.
Tu manes[3] ne laede meos, sed parce solutis
  Crinibus et teneris, Delia, parce genis.
Interea, dum fata sinunt, iungamus amores:
  Iam veniet tenebris mors adoperta[4] caput.

[1] ' *Bier,*' ' *funeral couch.*'
[2] *Here* = ' *eyes.*'
[3] *This plural noun means* ' *spirit.*'
[4] ' *Hooded,*' ' *covered.*'

VII

GENITIVE

The Latin genitive is commonly used:

1. *To express the dependence of one noun on another.*
EXAMPLES:

    (i) (Possessive) ' Regis causā.'
                    ' For the king's sake.'
    (ii) (Partitive) ' Satis cibi.'
                    ' Enough (of) food.'
    (iii) (Objective) ' Amor sciendi.'
                    ' Love of knowing.'
    (iv) (Quality) ' Vir summi ingenii.'
                    ' A man of the greatest ability.'

2. *To express the object of verbs of remembering, forgetting, and pitying.*
EXAMPLE:

              ' Epicuri non obliviscor.'
              ' I do not forget Epicurus.'

3. *After several adjectives.* Most of these represent adjectives which in English are followed by ' of ' (*e.g.* ' inscius ' = ' ignorant '), but note carefully the following: *avidus* (' greedy for . . . '), *studiosus* (' eager for . . . '), *particeps* (' sharing in . . .'), *expers* (' free from . . . '), and *peritus* (' skilled in . . . ').
EXAMPLE:

              ' Omnium vitiorum expers.'
              ' Free from all faults.'

4. *With verbs of buying, selling, and valuing,* to denote
PRICE or VALUE.

EXAMPLE:

> ' Hoc magni aestimo.'
> ' I value this highly.'

5. *With verbs of accusing, condemning, and acquitting,*
to denote the CHARGE.

EXAMPLE:

> ' Te furti accuso.'
> ' I accuse you of theft.'

6. *With esse, to denote the* NATURE *or* PROPERTY *of
some person or thing.*

EXAMPLE:

> ' Cuiusvis hominis est errare.'
> ' It is the nature of any man to make mistakes.'

7. *To denote the* LOCATIVE *case in the singular of the
first and second declensions.*

EXAMPLES:

> (i) ' Romae ' = ' at Rome.'
> (ii) ' humi ' = ' on the ground.'

[*Note.*—Some IMPERSONAL VERBS have constructions with the genitive: for these see chapter
XIII.]

Ulysses pretends to be mad, but does not deceive Palamedes.

Ulixes, vir summi ingenii, qui princeps erat Ithacae, multa et fortia ante muros Troiae agebat; primum tamen ad bellum ire nolebat, sociosque, qui auxilii petendi causā Ithacam venerunt, decipere constituit. Itaque, simulans se insanum esse neque amicorum meminisse, arare[1] harenam salemque[2] serere coepit. Sed inter socios erat Palamedes, qui omnium artium erat peritus: hic Ulixem fraudis accusavit et, ut hoc confirmaret, Telemachum, parvum filium Ulixis, humi ante aratrum posuit. Tum Ulixes, aratrum sistere coactus, ne filium occīderet, partes[3] insani agere desivit: neque enim est insani de re tali providere.

[1] ' *Aro* ' = ' *I plough.*' (*From this guess* ' *aratrum* ').

[2] ' *Sal* ' = ' *salt.*' *Remembering that Ulysses was doing useless things, you can guess any other words that you do not know here.*

[3] ' *Partes agere* . . .' = ' *to play the part* . . .'

Vercingetorix excites a revolt.

Vercingetorix, Celtilli filius, Arvernus, summae potentiae adulescens, cuius pater principatum Galliae totius obtinuerat, et ob eam causam, quod regnum adpetebat, ab civitate erat interfectus, convocatis suis clientibus, facile incendit[1]. Cognito eius consilio, ad arma concurritur. Prohibetur ab Gobannitione, patruo[2] suo, reliquisque principibus, qui hanc tentandam[3] fortunam non existimabant; expellitur ex oppido Gergovia; non desistit tamen, atque in agris habet dilectum egentium[4] ac perditorum[4]. Hortatur ut communis libertatis causa arma capiant, magnisque coactis copiis adversarios suos, a quibus paulo ante erat eiectus, expellit ex civitate.

[1] *You must supply the object of this transitive verb.*

[2] *' Uncle.'*

[3] *See XII. 1. (b).*

[4] *If you know ' egeo ' and ' perdo ' you should be able to understand these two adjectives, which were participles of those verbs.*

7 C

' Let us love while we may.'

Vivamus, mea Lesbia, atque amemus,
Rumoresque senum severiorum
Omnes unius aestimemus assis[1].
Soles occidere et redire possunt:
Nobis cum semel occidit brevis lux,
Nox est perpetua una dormienda.
Da mi basia[2] mille, deinde centum.
Dein mille altera, dein secunda centum,
Deinde usque altera mille, deinde centum.
Dein, cum milia multa fecerimus,
Conturbabimus[3] illa, ne sciamus,
Aut ne quis malus invidere possit,
Cum tantum sciat esse basiorum.

[1] *' As, assis ' = ' a penny.'*
[2] *' Kisses.'*
[3] *What does the ' turb- ' root mean?   Notice that the poet does not want an accurate account kept.*

37

VIII

DATIVE

1. The dative case, in many of its uses, can be translated by ' to ' or ' for ' : the English may then have to be improved.

(a) Indirect Object (but see III. 4., Examples, for some exceptions).

> EXAMPLE :
>> ' Librum mihi dederunt.'
>> ' They gave (*to*) me a book.'

(b) Possessor.

> EXAMPLE :
>> ' Mihi iam erant duo libri.'
>> [' There already were *to* me two books.']
>> ' I already had two books.'

(c) After certain adjectives.

> EXAMPLE :
>> ' Dixerunt librum mihi utilem fore.'
>> ' They said that the book would be useful to me.'

(d) Advantage (or Disadvantage).

> EXAMPLE :
>> ' Cur libros pueris scribunt ? '
>> ' Why do they write books *for* boys ? '

(e) Predicative.

> EXAMPLE :
>> ' Nemini liber talis est *usui*.'
>> [' Such a book is *for* a use to no-one.']
>> ' Such a book is of no use to anyone.'

(*f*) ' Work contemplated.'

EXAMPLE :

' Diem libro urendo dixi.'

' I have appointed a day *for* burning the book.'

2. There are two types of dative which cannot be translated by the English ' to ' or ' for ' (apart from the instances given in III. 4 (a) and its examples).

(*a*) The dative of the *agent*, used with *gerunds, gerundives* and, occasionally, *passives*.

EXAMPLE :

' Captivi nobis sunt occidendi.'

' The prisoners must be killed *by* us.'

(*b*) The dative denoting the object of verbs which in English are transitive but in Latin intransitive.

EXAMPLES :

(i) ' Hostibus pepercit.'
' He spared his enemies.'

(ii) ' Suis subveniunt.'
' They help their own men.'

Note.—For a complete list of these verbs you must consult a grammar : but you should already know *credo, faveo, fido, ignosco, noceo, parco, pareo, placeo, resisto, servio, (per)suadeo,* and their meanings. Many verbs compounded with *in-, ob-, prae-,* and *sub-* are followed by the dative : these must be learnt by experience. ' *Consulo* ' takes an *accusative* when it means ' *consult,*' and a *dative* when it means ' *consult the interests of.*'

The burning of the Sibylline books.

Antiquis temporibus, ut narratur, anus[1] incognita ad Tarquinium Superbum regem adiit, novem libros ferens, quos esse divina oracula dicebat; his rēgi traditis, pretium ingens poposcit.   Rex, quamquam putabat libros sibi esse obtinendos, tantam pecuniam dare nolebat.   Anus igitur tres libros regi ademit et, his incensis, idem pretium poposcit : sed regi, qui sex libros eodem pretio ac novem emere minimē[2] volebat, haud ita persuasit.   Itaque mulier statim tres alios libros incendit, regemque rogavit ut tres reliquos eodem pretio emeret.   Tum demum rex, tantā constantiā victus, anui paruit; nam, ratus utilissimum sibi esse oracula habere, tres reliquos libros tanti[3] emit quanti[3] anus omnes vendere voluerat.

[1] ' *Anus* ' = ' *old woman.* '
[2] ' *Very little* ' : *often* ' *not at all.* '
[3] *See VII. 4.*

Petronius, attacking the town of Gergovia, advises his men to save themselves and dies fighting.

M. Petronius, eiusdem legionis centurio, cum portas excidere conatus esset, a multitudine oppressus et sibi desperans, multis iam vulneribus acceptis, militibus suis qui illum secuti erant, ' Quoniam,' inquit, ' me una vobiscum servare non possum, vestrae quidem certe vitae prospiciam, quos cupiditate gloriae adductus in periculum deduxi. Vos, data facultate, vobis consulite.' Simul in medios hostes irrupit, duobusque interfectis reliquos a porta paulum submovit. Conantibus auxiliari suis, ' Frustra,' inquit, ' meae vitae subvenire conamini, quem iam sanguis viresque deficiunt. Proinde[1] abite dum est facultas vosque ad legionem recipite.' Ita pugnans post paulum concidit et suis saluti fuit.

[1] ' *Therefore.*'

The power of Time.

Tempore ruricolae patiens fit taurus aratri,
    Praebet et incurvo colla premenda iugo ;
Tempore paret equus lentis animosus habenis,
    Et placido duros accipit ore lupos[1] ;
Tempore Poenorum compescitur ira leonum,
    Nec feritas animo, quae fuit ante, manet,
Quaeque sui monitis obtemperat Inda magistri
    Belua, servitium tempore victa subit.
Tempus ut extensis tumeat facit uva racemis[2],
    Vixque merum capiant grana[3] quod intus habent.
Hoc tenuat dentem terram renovantis aratri,
    Hoc rigidas silices, hoc adamanta terit.
Hoc etiam saevas paulatim mitigat iras,
    Hoc minuit luctus maestaque corda levat.

[1] ' *Lupus* ' (*lit.* = ' *wolf* ') = ' *a bit* ' (*with points like wolves'*
teeth).

[2] ' *Racemus* ' = ' *cluster of grapes.* '

[3] *The seeds are so much swollen with the juice which is to be wine,*
that they can hardly contain it ; translate the Latin words into good
English.

ABLATIVE

1. The ablative without a preposition has many uses in Latin : some instances of the commonest will remind you what to expect.

EXAMPLES :

(i) (Instrument)

' Rex fratrem suum veneno necaverat.'

' The king had killed his brother by poison.'

(ii) (Measure)

' Iuvenis multō tristior quam antea fiebat.'

' The young man was becoming much sadder than before.'

(iii) (Separation)

' Nemo eum miseriis liberare poterat.'

' No one could free him from his distress.'

(iv) (Manner)

' Magnā curā fabulam paravit.'

' With great care he prepared a play.'

(v) (Cause)

' Rex, metū commotus, exiit.'

' The king, wild with fear, went out.'

(vi) (Description)

' Iuvenis adhuc incertō erat animō.'

' The young man was still uncertain in his mind ' (lit. ' with-uncertain-mind').

(vii) (Comparison)

> ' Se segniorem inimicis suis praebuit.'
> ' He showed himself slower than his enemies.'

(viii) (' Time within which ' and ' time when ')

> ' Paucis diebus mortui sunt omnes primo vespere.'
> ' In a few days they all died in the evening.'

2. The ablative regularly follows some **verbs** and some adjectives. The commonest are:—

' Utor '	= ' I use '	' Dignus '	= ' worthy of.'
' Fruor '	= ' I enjoy '	' Fretus '	= ' relying on.'
' Fungor '	= ' I perform '	' Orbus '	= ' deprived
' Potior '	= ' I get pos-		of '
	session of '	' Praeditus '	= ' endowed
' Careo '	= ' I lack '		with '

Note.—' Egeo ' (= ' I lack ' or ' need ') and ' plenus ' (= ' full of ') are followed by the ablative *or* genitive.

3. The ablative, like the genitive,

(*a*) Can express *price* or *value*. The ablative properly denotes a definite price, the genitive an indefinite price.

EXAMPLE :

> ' Id denario emi.'
> ' I bought it for eightpence.'

(*b*) Does duty for the *locative* case.

EXAMPLE :

> ' Ei Athenis occurri.'
> ' I met him at Athens.'

44

[*Note* that, with names of towns and small
islands, the ablative without a preposition
may also mean ' *from*.']

4. A participle phrase which has no grammatical
connection with the rest of its sentence goes into
the ablative (' Ablative Absolute').

EXAMPLE :
' Hīs rebus gestīs Curio se in castra recipit.'
' When he had done this, Curio retired to his
camp.'

Note.—Sometimes the participle is replaced by an
adjective or a second noun in this construction.

EXAMPLE :
' Consule Manlio '
' When Manlius was consul '

How the bear lost his tail : a legend.

Ursus olim, cum cibum hieme peteret, vulpem[1],
quae ei occurrit, rapuit : sed illa, callido[2] freta
ingenio, ' Noli me tangere,' inquit, ' nam pisces
cibum multo iucundiorem meā carne[3] tibi prae-
bebunt.'

' Quomodo pisces capiam ? '

' Nihil hōc facilius est. Ad lacum progressus,
glacie ruptā, caudam[4] tuam in aquam demitte. Hanc
pisces statim mordebunt. Tu tamen mane dum
multi adsint : tum caudā omnes de lacu tollere
poteris.'

Ursus, his verbis deceptus, caudā diu sic utebatur,
nec frigus, quod caudam summo dolore afficiebat,
aegre tulit, quia pisces se mordere credidit. Sed
tandem, cum pisces de aquā tollere vellet, caudam
non potuit movere : adeo glacie gelata erat, ut ibi
eam relinquere coactus sit.

[1] ' *Fox.*'
[2] ' *Callidus* ' = ' *cunning.*'
[3] ' *Caro* ' (*gen.* ' *carnis* ') = ' *flesh.*'
[4] *Guess this word from the heading.*

A most holy temple is robbed, but its sanctity is later respected.

Insula est Melita, iudices, satis lato ab Sicilia mari periculosoque disiuncta : in qua est eodem nomine oppidum.   Ab eo oppido non longe, in promontorio, fanum est Iunonis antiquum : quod tanta religione semper fuit, ut non modo illis [1] Punicis bellis, quae in his fere locis gesta sunt, sed etiam in hac[1] prae-donum multitudine semper inviolatum sanctumque fuerit.   Quin etiam [2] hoc memoriae proditum est, classe quondam Masinissae regis ad eum locum appulsa, praefectum regium dentes eburneos in-credibili magnitudine e fano sustulisse et eos in Africam portasse [3] Masinissaeque donasse [3].   Regem quidem primo delectatum esse munere : post, ubi audisset unde essent, statim certos homines in quinqueremi [4] misisse, qui eos dentes reportarent.

[1] ' *Ille* ' *here points to former times,* ' *hic* ' *to the present.*

[2] *See XIV. 2. (c).*

[3] *See XXVII. 1. (d).*

[4] *You may know a poem beginning* ' *Quinquereme of Nineveh . . .* ' *or be able to guess the meaning of this word from the two Latin words from which it is made up.*

Aeneas relates how he and the other Trojans, happy in the belief that the Greeks had gone, discovered the Wooden Horse.

Est in conspectu Tenedos, notissima fama
Insula, dives opum, Priami dum regna manebant;
Nunc tantum sinus et statio[1] male fida carinis.
Huc se provecti deserto in litore condunt.
Nos abiisse rati[2] et vento petiisse Mycenas:
Ergo omnis longo solvit se Teucria luctu;
Panduntur portae; iuvat ire et Dorica castra
Desertosque videre locos litusque relictum.
Hic Dolopum manus, hic saevus tendebat Achilles;
Classibus hic locus; hic acie certare solebant.
Pars stupet innuptae[3] donum exitiale Minervae,
Et molem mirantur equi; primusque Thymoetes
Duci intra muros hortatur et arce locari,
Sive dolo seu iam Troiae sic fata ferebant.

[1] ' *Anchorage.*' ' *Male fida* ' *should be taken together as* ' *treacherous.*'

[2] *After* ' *rati* ' *understand* ' *sumus,*' *and then* ' *eos.*'

[3] ' *Unmarried,*' ' *maiden.*'

X

INFINITIVE

1. *The infinitive may be used as the subject or complement of a sentence.*

EXAMPLE :

    ' Sapienti vivere est cogitare.'

    ' To a wise man living is thinking.'

2. *Many verbs complete their sense with a second verb in the infinitive.* As you get to know these verbs you will look for an infinitive after them.

(a) The commonest are verbs of *wishing, trying, resolving, beginning* and *ending :* very common also are the Latin verbs *possum* ('I am able'), *debeo* ('I ought'), *audeo* (' I dare ') and *soleo* (' I am accustomed ').

EXAMPLE :

    ' Pugnare non possum desistere.'

    ' I cannot stop fighting.'

(b) With other verbs the infinitive follows their objects (as in English) : the commonest are *iubeo* (' I order '), *veto* (' I forbid '), *cogo* (' I compel ') and *sino* (' I allow ').

EXAMPLE :

    ' Magister nos pugnare vetuit.'

    ' The master forbade us to fight.'

(c) Verbs of *seeming* and the passive of verbs of *saying* and *thinking* are followed by the infinitive : the Latin construction is usually personal, the English impersonal.

EXAMPLE :

> ' Socrates vir sapientissimus fuisse dicitur.'
> ' It is said that Socrates was very wise.'

Note.—Impersonal Verbs often complete their sense with the infinitive (or accusative and infinitive) : *see* Chapter XIII.

3. *An Indirect Statement is expressed in Latin by the accusative and infinitive.*

Note 1. You will find this after many verbs besides ' dico ' : it is a common construction after any verb which suggests the giving or receiving of information, and sometimes the verb itself has to be understood.

EXAMPLES :

> (i) ' Nesciebat Caesarem adesse.'
> ' He did not know that Caesar was present.'
> (ii) ' Dux litteras misit : se hostes vicisse . . .'
> ' The general sent a despatch : he said that he had conquered the enemy . . .'

Note 2. The Latin infinitive shows the speaker's tense, and, except after a primary verb, it cannot be translated by the same tense in English. See EXAMPLES (i) and (ii) above.

4. *An infinitive (known as the Historic Infinitive) is used as the main verb in vivid narrative.* Its subject remains in the nominative.

EXAMPLE :

> ' Hoc magis properare Varro.'
> ' For this reason Varro was in greater haste.'

A glorious death.

Fortiter mori pulcherrimum est : mori summam inter gloriam gratissimum[1]. Epaminondas igitur, Boeotorum imperator, ex omnibus ducibus felicissime putatur periisse. Illum enim, acie apud Mantineam instructā, mox agnoverunt Lacedaemonii : universi[2] impetum in unum facere, et, multis occisis, Epaminondam fortiter pugnantem hastā vulnerare : hostibus magnopere laetantibus[3], dux cadere. Huius casu paullum retardati[2] sunt Boeoti, nec tamen pugnare destiterunt. At Epaminondas, cum intellexisset se vulnus mortiferum[4] accepisse et, ferro extracto, statim moriturum esse, id retinuit dum renuntiatum est Boeotos vicisse. Quod cum audivisset, ' Satis,' inquit, ' vixi[5] : invictus enim morior.' Deinde ferrum suos extrahere iussit, nec multo post [6] periit.

[1] Supply the verb.

[2] Guess these from English words like them.

[3] ' Laetor ' is the verb of ' laetus.'

[4] ' Fatal ' or ' deadly.'

[5] Think carefully : does this come from ' vivo ' or ' vinco ' ? If you are in doubt remember Caesar's famous three words.

[6] ' Non multo post ' = ' not long afterwards.'

The Athenians reject a clever but dishonourable plan.

Themistocles post victoriam eius belli quod cum Persis fuit dixit in contione[1] se habere consilium rei publicae salutare[2], sed id sciri non opus esse; postulavit ut aliquem populus daret, quocum communicaret; datus est Aristides; huic ille, classem Lacedaemoniorum, quae subducta[3] esset ad Gytheum, clam incendi posse, quo facto frangi Lacedaemoniorum opes necesse esset. Quod Aristides cum audisset, in contionem magna exspectatione venit dixitque perutile esse consilium quod Themistocles adferret, sed minime honestum. Itaque Athenienses, quod[4] honestum non esset, id ne utile quidem[5] putaverunt, totamque eam rem, quam ne audierant quidem, auctore Aristide repudiaverunt.

[1] ' *Contio* ' = ' *assembly.* '
[2] *This is not an infinitive. What is it then?*
[3] ' *Subducere* ' = ' *to beach.* '
[4] *See XXIV. 2.*
[5] *See XIX. 1. (c).*

The poet declares that the order of the universe led men to invent gods and to imagine that their abode was in heaven.

Praeterea caeli rationes ordine certo
Et varia annorum cernebant tempora[1] verti,
Nec poterant quibus id fieret cognoscere causis.
Ergo perfugium[2] sibi habebant omnia divis
Tradere et illorum nutu[3] facere omnia flecti[4].
In caeloque deum[5] sedes et templa locarunt,
Per caelum volvi quia nox et luna videtur,
Luna, dies, et nox, et noctis signa severa,
Noctivagaeque[6] faces caeli flammaeque volantes,
Nubila, sol, imbres, nix, venti, fulmina, grando,
Et rapidi fremitus et murmura magna minarum[7].

[1] ' *Seasons.* '

[2] ' *Refuge.* ' *Early man, when faced with unknown forces, felt more comfortable when he thought of them as personal gods.*

[3] ' *Nutus* ' = ' *nod.* '

[4] ' *Flectere* ' *here* = ' *to control.* '

[5] *Genitive plural.*

[6] ' *Noctivagus* ' = ' *wandering by night.* '

[7] *This fine alliterative line describes thunder; you will not be able to translate it literally.*

XI

PARTICIPLES

1. **Meaning.**

Much difficulty is caused by a vague knowledge of the meaning of participles: to remind you therefore:—

The *present* and *future* participles in Latin are *active*.

The *perfect* participle is *passive*, EXCEPT in the case of *deponent* and *semi-deponent verbs*, which have *active* perfect participles.

' Amans ' = ' loving '; ' amaturus ' = ' about to love ' ; ' amatus ' = ' having been loved ' ; ' progressus ' = ' having advanced.'

2. **Translation.**

Bearing this in mind, always translate a participle *literally* first. This will often serve your purpose, especially if the participle is in the nominative. But often, having understood the meaning, you must express it differently in English.

(*a*) In most cases the use of ' *and* ' or ' *when* ' or *another English participle* will help you to translate the Latin into good English.

EXAMPLE :

' Gladio stricto praedam poposcit.'

[lit. : His sword having been drawn, he demanded the spoil.']

' He drew his sword *and* demanded the spoil.'

or ' *When* he had drawn his sword, he demanded the spoil.'

or ' *Having drawn* his sword, he demanded the spoil.'

(b) But in some cases the participle stands for a ' *qui* ' clause, a ' *si* ' clause, a ' *quamquam* ' clause, etc. Then you must bring this out in your translation.

EXAMPLE:

' Me pinnīs sectare datīs.'

[' Follow me on the having-been-given wings.']

' Follow me on the wings *which* I have given you.'

3. Order.

The participle usually stands at the end of its clause : this will help you to tell which Latin words belong to the main sentence and which to the participle phrase, even when there are no commas to help.

EXAMPLE:

' Quā re per exploratores cognitā summo labore Caesar flumen transiit.'

' Having learnt this by means of scouts, Caesar crossed the river with great difficulty.'

Words standing between a noun and the participle agreeing with it are almost always part of the participle clause.

EXAMPLE:

' Ab hostibus ad casum regis concitatīs confossus periit.'

' He was stabbed by enemies, who had rushed to the scene of the king's fall, and died.'

Note.—Order can be most helpful in prose, but it is less so in verse, since the words are arranged to fit the metre.

An unexpected reply.

Antiochus, rex Syriae, Poenis superatis Hannibalem apud se excepit. Ei ostendit copias in campo instructas, quas bellum populo Romano facturus comparaverat : milites, currūs, equos, elephantos monstravit, omnesque armis aureis sumptuosē ornati sunt. Tum rex, contemplatione tanti exercitūs elatus, Hannibalem aspexit et, ' Putasne,' inquit, ' haec omnia satis esse Romanis ? '   At Hannibal, ignaviam militum eius pretiosē armatorum aspernatus[1], respondit. ' Credo certē satis esse haec omnia Romanis, etiam si avarissimi[2] sunt.'   Rex de numero exercitūs sui quaesiverat ; respondit Hannibal de praedā.

[1] ' Aspernor ' = ' I despise.'
[2] ' Avarus ' = ' greedy.'

The end of Horatius' defence of the bridge against the Etruscan army.

Pudor deinde commovit aciem[1], et clamore sublato undique in unum hostem tela coniciunt. Quae cum in obiecto cuncta scuto haesissent, neque ille[2] minus obstinatus ingenti pontem obtineret gradu, iam impetu conabantur detrudere virum, cum simul fragor rupti pontis, simul clamor Romanorum, alacritate perfecti operis[3] sublatus, pavore subito impetum sustinuit. Tum Cocles, ' Tiberine pater ', inquit, ' te precor ut haec arma et hunc militem propitio[4] flumine accipias! ' Ita sic armatus in Tiberim desiluit, multisque superincidentibus[5] telis incolumis ad suos tranavit[5].

[1] *This refers to the Etruscans who have been hesitating.*

[2] ' *Ille* ' = ' *Horatius.*' *The ' non ' of ' neque ' goes with the* ' *minus.*'

[3] *This phrase is much compressed in Latin : when you see what it means, express it more fully in English.*

[4] ' *Propitius* ' = ' *favourable.*'

[5] *Notice the words that make up these compounds (super-incadere and trans-nare).*

Orpheus, leading his wife Eurydice up from Hades, looks round at her, forgetting Pluto's command, and loses her.

Iamque pedem referens casus evaserat omnes
Redditaque Eurydice superas veniebat ad auras
Pone[1] sequens—namque hanc dederat Proserpina
    legem—
Cum subita incautum dementia cepit amantem,
Ignoscenda[2] quidem, scirent si ignoscere Manes:
Restitit, Eurydicenque suam iam luce sub ipsa
Immemor heu! victusque animi[3] respexit. Ibi omnis
Effusus labor, atque immitis rupta tyranni
Foedera, terque fragor stagnis auditus Avernis.
Illa, ' Quis et me,' inquit, ' miseram et te perdidit,
    Orpheu,
Quis tantus furor? En iterum crudelia retro
Fata vocant conditque natantia[4] lumina somnus.'
Dixit et ex oculis subito, ceu fumus in auras
Commixtus tenues, fugit diversa.

[1] ' *Behind* ' (*adverb*).
[2] ' *Pardonable.*'
[3] *This is the locative case:* = ' *in his heart.*'
[4] ' *Swimming,*' *i.e.* ' *tearful.*'

XII

GERUND, GERUNDIVE, AND SUPINE

1. Some people fight shy of *gerunds and gerundives*, because they are not sure when to use one and when the other. But in unseens you will find that the Romans were not afraid to use them, and so you must know their meanings: on the other hand they did know when to use the gerund and when the gerundive, and so that side of things is settled for you. Try to see, however, for your prose-writing, why they now use the gerund and now the gerundive according to the rules given in your grammar. They have two different uses :—

(*a*) To represent *the English verbal noun in ' -ing.'*
EXAMPLES :

> (i) ' Ars libros scribendi ' (gerund).
> ' The art of writing books.'
> (ii) ' Libris scribendis ' (gerundive).
> ' By writing books.'

Note.—The Latin infinitive may also represent the English noun in ' -ing ' (*see* Chapter **X**, 1 and 2 (*a*)).

(*b*) To express *obligation*, i.e. *duty* or *necessity*, usually with a part of ' sum.'

If you are doubtful about the correct translation here, first translate the gerundive as an adjective meaning ' meet-to-be- —— ed.' Then express the meaning in good English.

EXAMPLES :

(i) ' Carthago delenda est.'
[' Carthage is meet-to-be-destroyed.']
' Carthage must be destroyed.'

(ii) ' Moriendum erit omnibus.'
[' It will be meet-to-be-died by all.']
or, [' There will be for all a dying.']
' All will have to die.'

Note 1. Look out for a dative of the agent, meaning ' by,' with this use.

Note 2. The gerundive after *do* and *curo* has a special meaning.

EXAMPLES :

(i) ' Librum L. Cossinio ad te perferendum dedi.'
' I gave the book to Lucius Cossinius to be taken to you.'

(ii) ' Naves aedificandas curat.'
' He has ships built.'

2. Few boys ever use *supines*, but again for unseens you must know their meanings. *Both can be translated by the English infinitive,* for

(*a*) The supine in ' -um ' expresses purpose after a verb of motion. The sense alone will show you that it is a supine, not a past participle.

EXAMPLE :

' Auxilium postulatum venerunt.'
' They came to ask for help.'

(*b*) The supine in ' -u ' depends on an adjective.

EXAMPLE :

' Difficile factū.'
' Difficult to do.'

A quarrel about an ass's shadow.

Demosthenes, ubi iudices occasionem loquendi ei dare nolebant, hanc fabulam narravit:

' Iuvenis, cui Megaram aestate mediā erat eundum, asinum conducendum[1] curavit: at, pauca milia passuum progressus, vitandi caloris causā sub umbrā asini cubitum[2] ire constituit. Asinarius tamen, quod[3] iuvenis nihil nisi asinum conduxisset, umbram adhuc esse suam adfirmavit.'

Tum iudices quomodo haec rixa componenda[4] esset rogaverunt: sed Demosthenes eos culpavit, quia de re gravissimā nihil audire voluerant sed cui tribuenda esset umbra asini scire sic cupiebant.

[1] ' *Conducere* ' = ' *to hire.* '
[2] ' *Cubo* ' = ' *I lie down,* ' ' *I sleep.* '
[3] *See XXIV.* 2.
[4] ' *Componere* ' = ' *to settle.* '

The character of Hannibal.

Missus Hannibal in Hispaniam primo statim adventu
omnem exercitum in se convertit[1] ; Hamilcarem[2]
iuvenem redditum sibi veteres milites credebant.
Dein brevi tempore effecit ut pater in se mini-
mum momentum[3] ad favorem conciliandum esset.
Nunquam ingenium idem ad res diversissimas,
parendum atque imperandum, habilius fuit. Itaque
haud facile discerneres utrum imperatori an exercitui
carior esset; neque Hasdrubal alium quemquam
praeficere malebat, ubi quid[4] fortiter ac strenue
agendum esset, neque milites alio duce plus confide-
bant aut audebant. Plurimum audaciae ad pericula
capessenda[5], plurimum consilii inter ipsa pericula
erat. Nullo labore aut corpus fatigari aut animus
vinci poterat.

[1] ' Converto ' here means ' turn the eyes of . . . towards. . . ' : how
will you express this in English ?

[2] Hamilcar was the father of Hannibal.

[3] ' Influence ' : the sentence means that his own qualities soon
became a stronger recommendation than his father's memory.

[4] See XXIII. 2.

[5] ' Capessere ' has 'capere' as its root.

Ovid describes the scene at his home on the night when he went into exile.

Quocunque adspiceres, luctus gemitusque sonabant,
    Formaque non taciti funeris intus erat.
Femina virque meo, pueri quoque, funere maerent ;
    Inque domo lacrimas angulus[1] omnis habet.
Si licet exemplis in parvo grandibus uti,
    Haec facies Troiae, cum caperetur, erat.
Iamque quiescebant voces hominumque canumque ;
    Lunaque nocturnos alta regebat equos.
Hanc ego suspiciens, et ad hanc[2] Capitolia cernens,
    Quae nostro frustra[3] iuncta fuere Lari :
' Numina vicinis habitantia sedibus,' inquam,
    ' Iamque oculis numquam templa videnda meis ;
Dique relinquendi, quos Urbs habet alta Quirini,
    Este salutati tempus in omne mihi[4].'

[1] *From this word comes the English ' angle.'*

[2] *' Ad hanc ' = ' by the light of the moon ' here.*

[3] *' Frustra ' : because its nearness to Ovid's house had not saved him.*

[4] *See VIII. 2. (a).*

IMPERSONAL VERBS

1. *Many impersonal verbs can be translated by the English ' it . . . '* and have constructions that are easily recognized.

EXAMPLES :

(i) ' Pluit ' = ' It rains.'

(ii) ' Constat hoc verum esse.'

' It is agreed that this is true.'

Note.—Distinguish between

' accidit ut . . . ' (' it happens that . . .') and ' accedit ut . . .' (' it happens in addition that . . . ')

2. *The verbs ' interest ' and ' refert ' are also translated by the English impersonal,* but their construction is curious.

EXAMPLE :

' Dixit non tam suā quam rei publicae interesse ut salvus esset.'

' He said that it was not so much to his own interest as to the state's that he should be safe.'

[*Note* that the party interested goes in the genitive, but that meā, tuā, suā, nostrā, vestrā are used instead of mei, tui, etc.]

3. *Impersonal verbs which express ' feeling ' are usually rendered personally in English.*

With *miseret, paenitet, piget, pudet* and *taedet,* the Latin accusative becomes the subject in English, and the Latin genitive (or infinitive) gives you the cause of the feeling (often the English object).

  (i) ' Eum latronis miseret.'

   ' He pities the robber.'

  (ii) ' Puerum taedet laboris.'

   ' The boy is tired of work.'

  (iii) ' Me id dixisse paenitet.'

   ' I am ashamed of having said that.'

4. *Some other Latin impersonals (followed by the infinitive) are also better translated personally in English.* Such are *iuvat* and *oportet* (+ *accusative*) : *licet* and *placet* (+ *dative*).

EXAMPLES :

  (i) ' Te oportuit manere.'

   ' You ought to have stayed.'

   [*Note* that English makes the *infinitive* past.]

  (ii) ' Nobis licet abire.'

   ' We are allowed to go away.'

  (iii) ' Eis placuit dictatorem creare.'

   ' They decided to appoint a dictator.'

Note.—It is assumed in the above paragraphs that impersonal verbs are not entirely new to you : look up the meaning of any that you do not already know.

5. *Impersonal passives in Latin present little difficulty.* They can usually be translated (i) by an English personal passive, (ii) by an active, or (iii) by an abstract.

EXAMPLES :

  (i) ' Mihi persuadetur.'

   ' I am persuaded.'

  (ii) ' A militibus fortiter pugnatum est.'

   ' The soldiers fought bravely.'

  (iii) ' Ad arma concurritur.'

   ' There is a rush to arms.'

How the commanders voted after the battle of Salamis.

Inter omnes constat Themistoclem omnium qui Graecos contra Persas duxerint sapientissimum fuisse : sed astutiae[1] eius ceteros duces pigebat. Cum apud Salaminam pugnatum esset, Graeci praemium proponebant ei qui dux fortissimus a ducibus iudicaretur. Tum omnes se hoc praemio maxime dignos censebant : sed omnibus nomen Themistoclis secundum scribere placuit. Itaque ceteris ducibus singulae sententiae dabantur, sed Themistocli plurimae : praemium igitur huic tradere eos oportuit.

[1] ‘ *Astutia* ’ = ‘ *craftiness* ’ (*hence the English* ‘ *astute* ’).

The difficulties which the Romans encountered when fighting the Britons.

Toto hoc in genere pugnae, cum sub oculis omnium ac pro castris dimicaretur, intellectum est nostros propter gravitatem armorum, quod neque insequi cedentes possent neque ab signis discedere [1] auderent, minus [2] aptos esse ad huius generis hostem. Praeterea equites magno cum periculo dimicabant, quod illi [3] etiam consulto [4] plerumque cedebant et, cum paulum ab legionibus nostros removissent, ex essedis [5] desilirent et pedibus dispari proelio contendebant. Accedebat huc ut numquam conferti [6] sed rari magnisque intervallis proeliarentur stationesque dispositas haberent, atque alios alii deinceps exciperent [7] integrique et recentes defatigatis succederent.

[1] ' *To depart from the standards,*' *means* ' *to break ranks.*'
[2] ' *Minus* ' *here means* ' *not.*'
[3] *The enemy charioteers.*
[4] ' *Deliberately.*'
[5] ' *Essedum* ' = ' *chariot.*'
[6] ' *In close formation.*'
[7] ' *Relieve.*'

13 C

Wealth without love is nothing.

Non opibus mentes hominum curaeque levantur:
    Nam Fortuna sua tempora lege regit.
Sit[1] mihi paupertas tecum iucunda, Neaera:
    At sine te regum munera nulla volo.
O niveam quae te poterit mihi reddere lucem[2]!
    O mihi felicem terque quaterque diem[2]!
At si, pro dulci reditu quaecumque voventur,
    Audiat[3] aversa non meus aure deus,
Nec me regna iuvant nec Lydius aurifer amnis
    Nec quas terrarum sustinet orbis opes.
Haec alii cupiant: liceat mihi paupere cultu[4]
    Securo cara coniuge posse frui.

[1] *See VI. 3.*

[2] *Accusative of exclamation.*

[3] *The poet treats the god's deafness to his vows as a ' remote possibility ' (present subjunctive), but makes the main verb present indicative.*

[4] *' Paupere cultu ' = ' in humble style.'*

CONNECTING PARTICLES

These particles are used so frequently in Latin to join one sentence to another that it is absurd to tackle an unseen without knowing them. All are, of course, indeclinable and therefore easy to recognize.

1. *Some are simple and have only one meaning.* Of these the following often are not known:—

Nam Enim } = ' for ' Etenim	Itaque	= 'and so
	Igitur } Ergo }	= ' therefore '
Quidem = ' indeed '	Etiam	
Praeterea = ' moreover '	Quoque } Nec non } = ' also '	
Dein } Deinde } = ' then,' 'next'	Item	
Interim } Interea } = ' meanwhile '	Tamen	= ' however '
	Verum	= ' but '

Note 1.—At enim }
     At   } often introduces an imaginary objection (' but someone may say . . .'). You may well find that it can be translated more shortly.

Note 2. Do not ever be so careless as to confuse :—
  ' quidem ' with ' quidam ' (' a certain . . . ').
  ' tamen ' with ' tandem ' (' at last . . .').
  ' nam ' with ' iam,' ' nunc ' ('now ').
  ' ergo ' with ' erga ' (' towards ').

2. *Some vary in meaning according to the context.*

(*a*) *Autem* and *vero* sometimes introduce a sentence *in contrast* to the previous one (translate as ' *but*,' ' *however* '), and at other times they *add a point* (translate as ' *now*,' ' *in fact*,' ' *and*').

Autem often has a meaning so slight that it is better left out in an English translation: the same is true of *quidem*.

(*b*) *Ceterum* usually means ' *for the rest*,' but sometimes (especially in Livy and Sallust) it means ' *but*.'

(*c*) *Immo* (often *immo vero*) and *quin* (often *quin etiam* or *quin et*) mean literally EITHER ' *yea even* ' OR ' *nay, rather* ': that is to say, they introduce a climax in the argument, either confirming or contradicting what has gone before.

When you have decided which they are doing (and note that *quin* more commonly *confirms*, *immo* more commonly *contradicts*), put them into English suitable to the passage you are translating: ' *moreover*,' ' *why*,' ' *nay*,' and ' *on the contrary*,' are often useful translations.

Note.——With these words (given in 2) you cannot follow a rule closely, but must translate according to the sense of the passage and your knowledge of English prose.

' *Hic*,' ' *is*,' ' *ille*,' and ' *idem*,' (declined normally) are often used to connect one sentence with another: so is ' *qui* ' (see Chapter XXII).

What do dreams about the future mean?

Saepe homines de rebus futuris per somnia docentur: at quid haec somnia significent non semper intellegere possunt.

Cursor[1], ad Olympia profecturus, in somnis curru quadrigarum[2] vehi visus est. Māne ergo duos interpretes consuluit. Quorum hic, ' Vinces,' inquit: ' id enim significat celeritas et vis equorum.' Ille vero : ' Vincēris : nam quattuor ante te cucurrerunt.'

Praeterea alius cursor nuntiavit se aquilam in somnis esse factum. Huic amicus : ' Vicisti; nulla enim avis aquilā vehementius volat.' Deinde alterum interrogavit : et is, ' Victus es,' inquit. ' Nam aquila, alias aves insectans[3], ipsa semper postrema est.'

[1] *This is the noun of ' curro.'*
[2] *' Currus quadrigarum ' = ' a four-horse chariot.'*
[3] *' Insector ' is a stronger form of ' in-sequor.'*

Respect for old age.

Lysandrum Lacedaemonium dicere aiunt solitum[1]
Lacedaemonem esse honestissimum domicilium senectutis ; nusquam enim tantum tribuitur aetati, nusquam
est senectus honoratior. Quin etiam memoriae
proditum est, cum Athenis ludis quidam in thea-
trum grandis natu venisset, in magno consessu locum
nusquam ei datum a suis civibus : cum autem ad
Lacedaemonios accessisset, qui, legati cum essent,
certo in loco consederant, consurrexisse omnes illi
dicuntur et senem sessum[2] recepisse ; quibus cum
a cuncto consessu plausus esset multiplex datus,
dixisse ex eis quendam Athenienses scire quae recta
essent sed facere nolle.

[1] *The accusative and infinitive construction (sometimes with ' esse '
omitted) is frequent in this piece.*

[2] *Supine of ' sedeo.'*

The folly of war and the blessings of peace.

Quis furor est atram bellis arcessere Mortem!
    Imminet et tacito clam venit illa pede.
Non seges est infra, non vinea culta, sed audax
    Cerberus et Stygiae navita[1] turpis aquae.
Quin potius laudandus hic est quem prole parata[2]
    Occupat in parva pigra senecta casa[3] :
Ipse suas sectatur oves, at filius agnos,
    Et calidam fesso comparat uxor aquam.
Sic ego sim, liceatque caput candescere[4] canis[5]
    Temporis et prisci facta referre senem.

[1] *Tr. ' ferryman ' : Charon is meant.*

[2] *' Proles ' = ' offspring,' ' children ' : ' parare ' literally means ' prepare,' but here means ' beget.'*

[3] *' Cottage.'*

[4] *Understand ' me ' as subject of ' candescere ' (= ' grow white ') and ' referre ' (= ' recount '). ' Caput ' is accusative of respect ; ' senem ' is in apposition to the understood ' me.'*

[5] *' Cāni ' = ' gray hairs.'*

HELP AND GUESSWORK

1. Heading.

The English heading at the top of an unseen is the most obvious help are given, and yet it is often neglected; it will give you the sense of the whole piece, and sometimes a word in it will help you out with a difficult passage. So *look back to it constantly* and make sure that your final translation agrees with what it says.

It may give you further help if you know something of *the incidents to which the heading refers.* For instance, if you find ' Desperate end of Catiline's conspirators ' at the head of your piece, you will know at once that reckless courage and death are likely to figure in the unseen : but, if you remember also that Catiline's conspiracy was finally crushed in a battle, you will have additional clues to the sense of the Latin.

2. Metre.

If you can scan Latin verse, you should always study the metre in a verse unseen; you may easily, for example, find two nouns and two adjectives, all ending in ' -a,' in one line : the scansion will make clear at once which are in the nominative and which in the ablative—and which adjective agrees with which noun. The marking of some long vowels in the ' A ' pieces of this book may show you how

useful such knowledge can be, and encourage you
to learn the common Latin metres.

3. Words of the same root.

If you do not know a word, consider what Latin
words you do know from the same root.   There are
snags here, for many Latin words look alike but have
quite different meanings (părĕre, pārēre, and părare,
for instance) ; but it is always worth trying, especially
with compound words.

Notice that in compound verbs

(i) The vowel ' a ' in the simple verb often
becomes ' i ' in the compound, as in ' desilio '
below.   Other changes are ' e ' to ' i '
('dirigo '), ' a ' to 'e ' (' perpetior '), and
' ae ' to ' i ' (' conquiro ').

(ii) The final letter of the prefix is often changed,
as in

afferre (ad-ferre)
auferre (ab-ferre)
corripere (con-rapere).

EXAMPLE :

' Saluti fuit eques, qui raptim ipse desiluit
pavidumque regem in equum subiecit.'

' Raptim ': you know ' rapio ' (supine ' raptum '
= ' snatch ').   Guess ' hurriedly ' therefore.

' Desilio ': ' de-' = ' down,' ' salio ' = ' jump.'
Therefore ' desilio ' = ' jump down ' or ' dis-
mount.'   [You might guess this from the rest
of the sentence anyway.]

' Pavidus ': you may know from ' paveo ' and
' pavor ' that ' pav-' denotes ' fear.'   Guess
' frightened.'

' Subiecit ' : clearly a compound of ' iacio ' =
' I throw.' The compound ' sub-' here (as
often) means *from* under, *i.e.* ' up.'
TRANSLATE :
' He was saved by a horseman, who himself dis-
mounted hurriedly, and set the terrified king on
his horse.'

4. **English words.**

Here again you may easily go astray, but, if you do
not know a word, it is worth seeing whether you
know an English word derived from it.   Remember
that, generally speaking, the longer English words are
derived from Latin, and many of them are taken from
the supines of verbs : therefore notice the conjuga-
tion of a verb you are trying to guess.   Times when
you may use this method with difficult words are
sometimes pointed out in the notes to this book, but
there are many other places where you can get help
from English.

5. **The sense of the passage.**

This is of course the main help in doing an unseen,
but *do not guess too early* : you will make many mistakes
if you jump to conclusions before the Latin has been
puzzled out.   Still, common sense is often your only
guide—for instance, when you are deciding in an
Indirect Statement which of the two accusatives is
subject, or translating an unknown word of which
you cannot discover the meaning by any of the
methods given above.   In your final version you
should *never leave blanks*.

Passages that look very difficult will become much
easier when you have read right through the piece

and found out what the simpler parts mean. It is remarkable how often the Romans (especially the poets) repeated themselves, or contrasted two obvious opposites : English does the same (particularly in the Prayer Book) and you must have noticed phrases like ' beg and beseech,' or ' comfort and succour,' in which the meaning of the second word was obvious to you from your knowledge of the first. Use the same method in Latin : notice parallel and contrasted words and phrases : study the connecting particle closely so that you know what relation a sentence bears to the one before it : and, above all, do not start writing till you have considered the whole passage and made sure that, whatever you show up, it is not nonsense.

A poet's defence.

Sophocles ad summam senectutem tragoedias fecit : cum propter hoc studium rem[1] familiarem neglegere videretur, a filiis in iudicium vocatus est. His enim pater ita desipiens[2] esse videbatur ut non iam rem[1] bene gerere posset; poscebant igitur a iudicibus ut bona patri[3] adempta filiis traderentur. Tum senex dicitur eam fabulam, quam in manibus habebat et proxime scripserat, Oedipum Coloneum) recitavisse iudicibus, et rogavisse num illud carmen desipientis videretur. Quo recitato, sententiis iudicum est liberatus.

[1] *Latin phrases with ' res ' cannot be so simply rendered in English : decide what is meant here and then express the meaning in good English.*

[2] *' Desipiens ' = ' de-sapiens ' (i.e. the opposite of ' sapiens ').*

[3] *See III 4. and then think.*

Thoughts on a voyage.

Ex Asia rediens cum ab Aegina Megaram versus[1] navigarem, coepi regiones circumcirca prospicere. Post me erat Aegina, ante me Megara, dextra Piraeus, sinistra Corinthus, quae oppida quodam tempore florentissima fuerunt, nunc prostrata et diruta ante oculos iacent. Coepi ego mecum sic cogitare: ' Hem! nos homunculi[2] indignamur, si quis nostrum interiit aut occisus est, quorum vita brevior esse debet, cum uno loco tot oppidorum cadavera[3] proiecta iacent? Visne tu te, Servi, cohibere et meminisse hominem te esse natum? ' Crede mihi, cogitatione ea non mediocriter sum confirmatus.

[1] ' *Towards.*'
[2] ' *Homunculus* ' *is a diminutive of* ' *homo.*'
[3] ' *Ruins* ' (*lit.* ' *corpses* ').

15 C

Ovid's schooldays and early love of poetry.

Protinus excolimur[1] teneri, curaque parentis
    Imus ad insignes Urbis ab arte viros,
Frater ad eloquium viridi tendebat ab aevo,
    Fortia verbosi natus ad arma fori ;
At mihi iam puero caelestia sacra[2] placebant,
    Inque suum furtim Musa trahebat opus.
Saepe pater dixit, ' Studium quid inutile temptas ?
    Maeonides[3] nullas ipse reliquit opes.'
Motus eram dictis, totoque Helicone[4] relicto
    Scribere temptabam verba soluta modis.
Sponte sua carmen numeros veniebat ad aptos,
    Et quod temptabam scribere, versus erat.

[1] ' *Excolere* ' = ' *educate.* '

[2] *Poetry was thought to be a holy calling—' caelestia sacra.'*

[3] *Homer.*

[4] *Helicon, the mountain of the muses, represents poetry ; you can guess what ' verba soluta modis ' stands for.*

PART II

XVI

UT

1. '*Ut,*' *followed by the indicative,* usually introduces a subordinate clause and means '*as*' or '*when.*'

EXAMPLES:

(i) 'Ita faciam ut mones.'

'I will do as you advise.'

(ii) 'Ut ad montes ventum est, castra posuerunt.'

'When the mountains were reached, they pitched camp.'

But sometimes 'ut' is used *with the main verb,* meaning '*how*'; the exclamation mark at the end will help you here.

EXAMPLE:

'Ut me malus abstulit error!'

'How the fatal madness carried me away!'

Note.—The compounds '*velut,*' '*sicut,*' and '*prout,*' are often used as stronger forms of '*ut*' meaning '*as,*' sometimes without a verb.

2. '*Ut,*' *followed by the subjunctive,* is more familiar. It is commonly used to express:—

(*a*) *Purpose.*

EXAMPLE:

'Londinium iit ut reginam videret.'

'He went to London, in order to see the queen.'

(*b*) *Consequence.*

Words like 'tam,' 'tantus,' and 'ita' will

81

often act as pointers here, showing you that the
' ut ' which follows is consecutive.

EXAMPLE :

> ' Tantus erat clamor ut nemo consulem
> audiret.'

> ' So great was the noise that nobody heard
> the consul.'

(c) *Command, Request, etc.*

After verbs like ' *impero*,' ' *peto*,' ' *hortor* ' and
' *persuadeo*,' the ' ut ' clause completes the sense
by telling us what the command (or request or
whatever it may have been) was.   Translate it
by the English infinitive.

EXAMPLES :

> (i) ' Ab eis petii ut mecum venirent.'
> ' I asked them to come with me.'
> (ii) ' Ei persuadebimus ut cantet.'
> ' We will persuade him to sing.'

These are not the only uses of ' ut ' with the subjunctive, but common sense usually makes the
meaning clear ;   notice the following :—

> (i) ' Ut desint vires, tamen est laudanda voluntas.'
> ' *Though* your strength is insufficient, yet
> your purpose is praiseworthy.'
> (ii) ' Vides ut alta stet nive candidum Soracte. '
> ' You see *how* Mount Soracte with its deep
> snow stands out white.'
> (iii) ' Sol efficit ut omnia floreant.'
> ' The sun causes everything to blossom.'
> (iv) 'Accidit ut non nulli milites interciperentur.'
> ' It happened *that* some soldiers were cut off.'

Note.—' *Uti* ' is often used for ' *ut* ' and must not
be confused with ' ūti,' meaning ' to use.'

King Mycerinus is ill-rewarded for his justice.

Mycerinus, ut dicitur, rex Aegyptiorum factus, nuntios ad oraculum Iovis misit, uti deum rogaret, ' Quot annos vivam ? ' Deus respondit Mycerinum, cum sex annos regnavisset, subito periturum esse. Sed ille, his verbis attonitus[1], ' Ut me di fraudant! ' inquit, ' nam pater et avunculus meus, qui populum multis iniuriis opprimebant, diu vixerunt; mihi tamen, ut tantā probitate[2] regam, Iuppiter vitam brevissimam tribuit.' Tum nuntiis imperavit ut a deō peterent cur pietatem ita puniret: nuntiatum est deum iratum esse, quod ipse decrevisset[3] Aegyptios summā crudelitate centum annos ad-flictum iri. Itaque Mycerinus, omni spe diu vivendi abiectā, multas lacernas[4] paravit ut per noctes, sicut per dies, conviviis[5] perpetuis frueretur; nam, ' Hoc modo,' inquit, ' ego deos decipiam et sex annos ab eis datos sic duplicabo.[6] '

[1] ' *Astonished.*'
[2] ' *Goodness.*'
[3] ' *Decerno, -ere, decrevi, decretum* ' = ' *decree.*'
[4] ' *Lanterns.*'
[5] ' *Feasts* ' (*hence our word* ' *convivial* ').
[6] *Think of the English word* ' *duplicate.*'

Curio's forces, defeated and trapped in Africa, panic with the result that few escape.

Marcius Rufus quaestor in castris relictus a Curione, ut de his rebus nuntiatum est, cohortatus est suos ne animo deficerent. Illi orant atque obsecrant, ut in Siciliam navibus reportentur. Pollicetur, magistrisque imperat navium, ut primo vespere omnes scaphas[1] ad litus appulsas habeant. Sed tantus fuit omnium terror ut alii adesse copias Iubae dicerent, alii cum legionibus instare Varum iamque se pulverem venientium cernere (quarum rerum nihil omnino acciderat), alii classem hostium celeriter advolaturam suspicarentur. Itaque perterritis omnibus sibi quisque consulebat[2], et tandem accidit ut pauci milites in Siciliam incolumes pervenirent.

[1] ' *Boats.*'
[2] *See VIII.* 2. (*b*), *Note.*

Ariadne, abandoned by Theseus, has her grief changed to fear by the arrival of Bacchus and his revelling followers.

Iamque iterum tundens mollissima pectora palmis
    ' Perfidus ille abiit.   Quid mihi fiet ? ' ait.
' Quid mihi fiet ? ' ait.   Sonuerunt cymbala toto
    Litore et attonita[1] tympana pulsa manu.
Excidit illa metu rupitque novissima[2] verba ;
    Nullus in exanimi corpore sanguis erat.
Ecce Mimallonides sparsis in terga capillis,
    Ecce leves satyri, praevia turba dei,
Ebrius ecce senex pando[3] Silenus asello
    Vix sedet et pressas continet ante iubas[4] :
Iam deus in curru, quem summum texerat uvis,
    Tigribus adiunctis aurea lora dabat.
Et color et Theseus et vox abiere puellae
    Terque fugam petiit terque retenta metu est ;
Horruit, ut steriles agitat quas ventus aristas[5],
    Ut levis in madida canna[6] palude tremit.

[1] ' *Wild.*'
[2] ' *Latest.*'
[3] ' *Pandus*' = ' *bent*' (*here with weight*).
[4] ' *Iubae*' = ' *mane.*'
[5] ' *Ears of corn.*'
[6] ' *Reed.*'

XVII

CUM AND DUM

These two words have several possible meanings ; in Unseens treat them as follows :

> (i) *First note whether the verb of the clause they introduce is indicative or subjunctive.* Some possible meanings of ' cum ' or ' dum ' can then be rejected in the passage you are considering.

> (ii) Then decide *from the sense of the passage* which of the meanings that are still possible is right.

1. **Cum.**

' *Cum* ' (*often written* ' *quum* ') *when used as a conjunction to introduce a subordinate clause* :

> (*a*) if it means *when,* is followed by *indicative or subjunctive* : as a rule primary tenses are indicative, historic are subjunctive ;

> (*b*) if it means *since, because,* is followed by the *subjunctive* ;

> (*c*) if it means *although, whereas,* is followed by the *subjunctive* ;

> (*d*) if it means *whenever* is followed by the *indicative* ;

> (*e*) if it means *since the time when* is followed by the *indicative.*

EXAMPLES :

(i) ' Cum hoc cognovissem, profectus sum.'
' When I had learnt this, I set out.'

(ii) ' Cum hoc sciat, iratus est.'
' Since he knows this, he is angry.'

(iii) ' Multi sunt anni cum hoc cognovi.'
' It is many years since (the time when) I learnt this.' ·

Note 1. ' *Cum* ' *followed by* ' *tum* ' is often used to connect two words or phrases in much the same way as ' et . . . et . . .' Translate as ' *both* . . . *and* . . .,' or ' *as* . . . *so* . . .,' or ' *not only* . . . *but also* . . .'

EXAMPLE :

' Sententia cum vera tum honesta visa est.'
' The opinion seemed not only true but also honourable.'

Note 2. ' *cum*,' *when used as a preposition with the ablative,* can almost always be rendered by the English '*with* ' : but it sometimes denotes ' attendant circumstances ' and is better translated as ' *amid* ' or ' *to*.'

EXAMPLE :

' Cum magno provinciae periculo . . .'
' To the great danger of the province . . .'

2. **Dum.**

' Dum,' *which is always used as a conjunction to introduce a subordinate clause* :

(*a*) if it means *until*, is followed by the *subjunctive* when referring to something *expected to happen*,

and by the *indicative* when referring to something *which has happened*;

(b) if it means *while*, is followed by the *indicative*;
(and the *present* tense of it, when the meaning
is ' *during the time while* ');

(c) if it means *provided that . . ., so long as . . .*,
is followed by the *subjunctive:* if the clause is
negative, ' *ne* ' is used rather than ' *non.*'

Note 1. ' *donec* ' and ' *quoad* ' are often used for
' *dum* ' in (a) and (b), and the strengthened form
' *dummodo* ' is very common in (c).

Note 2. You must learn
' *nondum* ' (adverb), which means ' *not yet,*' and
' *nedum* ' (conjunction), which means ' *much less . . .* '
                                or ' *not to say . . .* '

EXAMPLES :

(i) ' Dummodo ne moretur, manebo dum
veniat.'
' Provided that he does not delay, I will
wait till he comes.'

(ii) ' Puer nondum fert libertatem, nedum
dominationem.'
' The boy is not yet fit for freedom, and
much less for power.'

A cunning method of avoiding blame for a defeat.

Hannibal cum pugnā navali a Romanis victus esset,
non exspectavit dum a Poenis culparetur, sed unum ex
amicis suis fraudis[1] tentandae causā Carthaginem statim
misit.   Hic, urbem ingressus, cum sciret Hannibalem
iam superatum esse, eos qui rei Punicae praeerant
tamquam[2] de proelio nondum suscepto consuluit.
Nam, ' Quid censetis ? ' inquit.   ' Oportetne Hannibalem ducentīs cum navibus centum viginti naves
Romanas aggredi ? '   Omnes clamaverunt Hannibali
pugnandum esse dum navibus ne inferior esset hostibus.
Tum ille, ' Multi dies iam sunt cum pugnatum est :
Hannibal, victus, veniam petit a vobis qui proelium
committere eum modo iussistis.''

[1] *If you do not know 'fraus,' guess it from the story and from an
English word like it.*

[2] *See XXV. note 2.*

The ' wooden walls ' of Athens.

Cum Xerxes et mari et terra bellum universae inferret Europae cum tantis copiis, quantas neque ante nec postea habuit quisquam, magnopere trepidabatur : huius enim classis mille et ducentarum navium longarum fuit, quam duo milia onerariarum sequebantur ; terrestres autem exercitus DCC peditum[1], equitum CCCC milia fuerunt. Athenienses igitur, cum se maxime peti propter pugnam Marathoniam intellegerent, miserunt Delphos consultum[2], quidnam facerent de rebus suis.

Deliberantibus Pythia respondit ut moenibus ligneis se munirent. Id responsum quo valeret cum intellegeret nemo, Themistocles persuasit consilium esse Apollinis ut in naves se suaque conferrent : eum enim a deo significari murum ligneum.

[1] *This genitive shows that ' milia ' must be taken with DCC as well as with CCCC.*

[2] *Supine of ' consulo.'*

The poet complains that, while flattering a man from whom he hoped for a dinner, he has wasted time in which he might have written verse.

> Dum te prosequor et domum reduco,
> Aurem dum tibi praesto garrienti[1],
> Et quidquid loqueris facisque laudo,
> Quot versus poterant, Labulle, nasci!
> Hoc damnum tibi non videtur esse,
> Si quod Roma legit, requirit hospes,
> Non deridet eques, tenet senator[2],
> Propter te perit (hoc, Labulle, verum est).
> Hoc quisquam ferat? Ut tibi tuorum
> Sit maior numerus togatulorum[3],
> Librorum mihi sit minor meorum?
> Triginta prope iam diebus una est
> Nobis pagina vix peracta. Sic fit,
> Cum cenare domi poeta non vult.

[1] ' *Garrire* ' = ' *chatter* ' (*cf. English* ' *garrulous* ').

[2] *These two lines stress the demand at Rome for the writer's poetry.*

[3] *The* ' *toga* ' *was at this time mainly worn by* ' *clients* ' *of a rich man:* ' *-ulus* ' *is a diminutive implying* ' *little* ' *or* ' *petty.* '

XVIII

SI

Anyone can translate the word ' si ' as ' if,' but its constructions and the words formed from it need attention.

1. ' *Si* ' *regularly introduces a conditional clause.*

(*a*) When ' si ' is followed by the *indicative*, use the English equivalents of the Latin tenses.

(*b*) When ' si ' is followed by the subjunctive, there will be a ' *should* ' or ' *would* ' in the main sentence in English. For the force of the different tenses consult your grammar.

Note 1.

> ' *Nisi* ' and ' *ni* ' (' unless '),
> ' *etsi* ' (' even if,' ' although '),
> ' *sin* ' (' but if '),

and ' *quod si* ' ('and if ' or ' but if ')
take the same construction as ' si.'

' *Quasi* ' (' as if ') sometimes takes the construction of ' si,' but sometimes it only modifies a bold word or phrase, and means ' *almost* ' or ' *as it were.*'

Note 2. ' *Si non,*' without a verb, means ' *if not* ' or ' *otherwise.*'

EXAMPLES :

> (i) ' Si quando uxorem ducat, filiam cauponis deligat.'
>
> > ' If ever he married a wife, he would choose a landlord's daughter.'

(ii) ' Sin caelebs esse malet, siti quasi cruci-
abitur.'

' But if he prefers (lit. shall prefer) to be
single, he will be almost tormented
with thirst.'

2. *The historians often use a ' si ' clause to denote an
intention.* In these cases *si* must be translated as ' *to
see if* '.

EXAMPLE :

' Castra movit si potiri oppido posset.'

' He moved his camp to see if he could take
the city.'

3. ' *sive . . . sive . . .* ' (or ' *seu . . . seu . . .* ')
clauses are used in two ways.

(i) *When each ' sive ' clause has its own main
sentence,* the meaning is ' *if, on the one hand
. . . if, on the other . . .* '

(ii) *When one main verb serves both,* the meaning is
' *whether . . . or . . .* '

EXAMPLES :

(i) ' Sive lautum colit victum, opibus planē
abundat : sive non, pecuniam coacervare
habetur.'

' If he has a luxurious style of living, he
is obviously wealthy : but if not, he is
thought to be hoarding money.'

(ii) ' Sive igitur locuples sive pauper esse
videtur, vectigalia pendere cogitur.'

' So whether he seems to be rich or poor,
he is forced to pay taxes.'

93

The importance of omens.

Inter Romanos multa et magna ex ominibus pendebant[1]. Mos erat eis qui augurii erant periti aves spectare, si forte quid di vellent hoc modo reperirent: et, sive de foedere sive de proelio agebatur[2], consules voluntati deorum ita monstratae parēre solebant. Claudius tamen, cui quondam mandata est classis Romana, cum nuntiatum esset pullos[3] se cibo abstinere—quod res adversas planē significabat,— spreto omine, ' Si pasci nolunt,' inquit, ' iam bibant.' Quo dicto imperavit ut pulli in mare iacerentur : dein, classibus sine morā concurrentibus, Romani cladem acceperunt.

[1] *An English compound of ' -pend ' will translate ' pendere ' here.*
[2] *' Agitur de . . .' = ' it is a question of . . .'*
[3] *' Chickens.'*

Cyrus speaks on his deathbed of the immortality of the soul.

' Nolite arbitrari, o mihi carissimi filii, me, cum a vobis discessero, nusquam aut nullum fore. Nec enim, dum eram vobiscum, animum meum videbatis, sed eum esse in hoc corpore ex eis rebus quas gerebam intellegebatis. Eundem igitur esse creditote[1], etiam si nullum videbitis. Nec vero clarorum virorum post mortem honores permanerent, si nihil eorum ipsorum animi efficerent, quo[2] diutius memoriam sui teneremus. Mihi quidem nunquam persuaderi potuit animos, dum in corporibus essent mortalibus, vivere, cum excessissent ex eis, emori. Quare, si haec ita sunt, sic me colitote[1] ut deum; sin una est interiturus animus cum corpore, vos tamen deos verentes, qui hanc omnem pulchritudinem tuentur et regunt, memoriam nostri pie inviolateque servabitis.'

[1] *Imperative.*
[2] *See XXVI. 1. (iii).*

The servants who are casting Romulus and Remus adrift in a small boat guess from their appearance that they are the children of a god.

Huc ubi venerunt—neque enim procedere possunt
  Longius—ex illis unus et alter ait:
' At quam sunt similes! at quam formosus uterque!
  Plus tamen ex illis iste vigoris habet.
Si genus arguitur vultu, nisi fallit imago,
  Nescio quem[1] vobis suspicor esse[2] deum.
At si quis vestrae deus esset originis auctor,
  In tam praecipiti tempore ferret opem:
Ferret opem certe, si non ope mater egeret[3],
  Quae facta est uno mater et orba die.
Nata simul, moritura simul, simul ite sub undas,
  Corpora! ' Desierat, deposuitque sinu.

[1] *See XXIII. 1. note 1.*

[2] *Something must be supplied here in the English: the heading will tell you what.*

[3] *The ancients believed that a god could not be in two places at once.*

XIX

NE

1. ' *Ne* ' *is used as an adverb meaning* ' *not* ' :—

(*a*) In prohibitions, and sometimes in wishes (ch. VI. 1 and 4).

(*b*) In ' *dum* ' and ' *dummodo* ' clauses (ch. XVII. 2).

(*c*) In the phrase ' *ne . . . quidem* ' meaning ' *not even . . .* ' or ' *not . . . either.* '

EXAMPLE :

' Ne sues quidem id velint.'

' Not even the pigs would want that.'

2. ' *Ne* ' *is used as a conjunction for* ' *ut non* ' :—

(*a*) In indirect commands (tr. ' *not to . . .* ').

(*b*) In final clauses, and after verbs denoting care or precaution (tr. ' *that . . . not . . .* ').

(*c*) After verbs of fearing (tr. ' *that . . .* ').

(*d*) After verbs of preventing (tr. ' *from . . .* ').

EXAMPLE :

' Cave ne quis appropinquet.'

' Take care that no one approaches.'

Note 1. The word ' *lest,* ' though a possible translation of ' ne ' in (*b*) and (*c*), is not much used nowadays.

Note 2. ' *Neve* ' and ' *neu* ' are used in Latin instead of ' *et ne.* '

3. ' -ne ' *is sometimes added to the first word of direct and indirect questions.* This cannot be confused with the other uses of ' ne ' : in direct questions it is not translated; in indirect the English ' whether ' is its equivalent.

As it is properly written without a hyphen, it sometimes makes a word look unfamiliar for a moment, like the other ' enclitics,' ' -que ' (' and ') and ' -ve ' (' or ').

EXAMPLE :

> ' Tune ille Aeneas . . . ? '
> ' Are you that great Aeneas . . . ? '

4. ' Ne ' *is occasionally used with a personal pronoun to mean ' truly ' or ' indeed.'* This is a different word (and not a very common one) but it can be very perplexing in an unseen if you do not know of it.

EXAMPLE :

> ' Ne ego homo infelix fui.'
> ' I was indeed an unlucky man.'

A philosopher's indifference to the fate of his body.

Diogenes, vitam mollem diu aspernatus, amicis imperavit ut se mortuum proicerent neve ullā afficerent sepulturā[1]. Sed illi: 'Nonne times ne corpus tuum canes lanient[2]? Visne volucribus et feris cibum ita praebere?' Quibus philosophus, ut hunc timorem stultum esse ostenderet, 'Minimē,' inquit: 'sed vos baculum meum, quo omnes abigam[3], propter me ponite.' Tum amici: 'Quid proderit baculus? vel quomodo hoc ūti poteris? Non enim senties.' Et ille, 'Ne feras quidem sentiam. Quid igitur mihi erit, si cadaver laniabitur?'

[1] *When you see what this means literally, you must put it into good English.*

[2] *'Laniare'* = *'to tear.'*

[3] *This is a compound of 'ago.'*

Catiline heartens his men by telling them that bravery is best, even in defeat.

' In fuga salutem sperare, cum arma, quibus corpus tegitur, ab hostibus averteris, ea[1] vero dementia est. Semper in proelio iis maximum est periculum qui maxime timent : audacia pro muro habetur[2]. Cum vos considero, milites, et cum facta vestra aestimo, magna me spes victoriae tenet : animus, aetas, virtus vestra me hortantur ; praeterea necessitudo, quae etiam timidos fortes facit. Nam ne multitudo hostium circumvenire queat[3], prohibent angustiae[4] loci. Quod si virtuti vestrae fortuna inviderit[5], cavete ne inulti[6] vitam amittatis ; sed, virorum more[7] pugnantes, cruentam atque luctuosam victoriam hostibus relinquite.'

[1] *This word refers back to the first four words of the extract, and is he subject.*

[2] *Tr. ' serves.'*

[3] *' Queo ' = ' I am able.'*

[4] *' Narrowness.'*

[5] *Tr. ' grudges the victory.'*

[6] *' Unavenged.'*

[7] *' More ' + gen. = ' like,' 'in the manner of.'*

Gallus thinks with longing of the songs and the way of life of Arcadian shepherds: he also addresses his love and laments her absence.

Tristis at ille, ' Tamen cantabitis, Arcades,' inquit,
' Montibus haec vestris ; soli cantare periti
Arcades.   O mihi tum quam molliter ossa quiescant,
Vestra meos olim si fistula[1] dicat amores.
Atque utinam ex vobis unus vestrique fuissem
Aut custos gregis aut maturae vinitor uvae.
Hic gelidi fontes, hic mollia prata, Lycori,
Hic nemus ; hic ipso[2] tecum consumerer aevo.
Nunc insanus amor duri me Martis in armis
Tela inter media atque adversos detinet hostes :
Tu procul a patria (nec sit mihi credere tantum)
Alpinas, a! dura, nives et frigora Rheni
Me sine[3] sola vides.   A! te ne frigora laedant!
A! tibi ne teneras glacies secet aspera plantas[4].'

[1] ' *Pipe.*'

[2] ' *Ipse* ' *often cannot be translated by* ' *-self* ' : *here it means* ' *nothing but* . . .'

[3] ' *Sine* ' *governs* ' *me.*'

[4] ' *Feet.*'

ET, ATQUE, AC

1. With their regular meaning, ' *and*,' these three words present no difficulty. But you must always decide from the context whether they are coupling a new sentence, a new clause, or merely a new word, to what has gone before.

Note 1. In poetry these words sometimes stand second, or even third, in the sentence they are introducing.

Note 2. ' *At* ' does NOT mean ' *and*.'

2. ' *Et* ' is sometimes used like ' *etiam* ' to mean ' *too*,' ' *also*,' or ' *even*.' Look out for one of these uses when the sense tells you that ' and ' cannot be right.

3. ' *Et* . . . *et* . . .' (and in poetry ' *-que* . . . *-que* ') often mean ' *both* . . . *and* . . .' Here again the sense makes ' and . . . and . . .' obviously wrong, but careless boys do write it. (Compare ' *alii* . . . *alii* . . .' where the second ' alii ' means ' *others*,' but the first must be translated as ' *some* ').

4. After ' *par*,' ' *idem*,' ' *aequus*,' ' *similis*,' ' *dis-*, *similis*,' ' *alius*,' ' *contra*,' and ' *secus*,' ' atque ' and ' ac ' (and sometimes ' et ') denote comparison.

They must be translated here by ' *as*,' ' *to*,' ' *from*,' or ' *than*,' according to the context.

EXAMPLES :

      (i) ' Pariter patribus ac plebi carus.'

        ' As dear to the senate as to the people.'

     (ii) ' Illi sunt alio ingenio ac tu.'

        ' They are different from you in character.'

Note.—' *Simul atque* ' and ' *simul ac* ' regularly mean ' *as soon as*.'

' Great Pan is dead.'

Navis oneraria, ut dicitur, eis insulis quae Echi-
nades appellantur appropinquabat, cum vox ab orīs
reddita subito clamavit, ' Thamou! Thamou! '
Gubernator, cui nomen erat Thamous, primum
tacebat: deinde, brevi responso dato, haec verba
audiit: ' Cum ad proximas insulas pervēneris,
nuntiā dum praeteris[1] Pana potentem periisse.'
Quo audito, omnes stupebant; nam et Thamous
ignorabat quid hoc mandatum significaret. Fiebat
inter nautas multus sermo: ac tandem placuit[2], si
vento uterentur secundo, nihil dicere, at, si serena
esset tempestas, mortem dei nuntiare. Et simul
atque ad insulas pervenerunt, tanta subito malacia[3]
ac tranquillitas exstitit ut navis se movere non posset.
Thamous igitur eadem verba atque audierat emisit:
' Pan potens periit.' Et continuo tota insula clamore
fletuque resonabat; et ferae et arbores dominum
suum lugere videbantur.

[1] *From ' praeter-eo.'*
[2] *See XIII. 4.*
[3] *Guess this uncommon word from ' tranquillitas ' (XV. 5.).*

The death of the consul Flaminius at Trasimene.

Tres ferme horas pugnatum est, et ubique atrociter. Circa consulem tamen acrior infestiorque pugna est. Eum et robora virorum sequebantur, et ipse, quacumque in parte premi ac laborare senserat suos, impigre[1] ferebat opem; insignemque[2] armis et hostes summa vi petebant et tuebantur cives: donec Insuber eques (Ducario nomen erat) facie quoque noscitans[2], 'Consul, en,' inquit, ' hic est,' popularibus suis, ' qui legiones nostras cecidit, agrosque et urbem est depopulatus. Iam ego hanc victimam manibus peremptorum[3] foede civium dabo.' Subditisque[4] calcaribus equo, per confertissimam[5] hostium turbam impetum facit : obtruncatoque prius armigero, qui se infesto venienti obviam obiecerat, consulem lancea transfixit.

[1] *If ' piger ' means ' idle,' what does this mean ?*

[2] *Supply ' consulem ' or ' eum.'*

[3] *' Perimo ' = ' kill.' You will have to be careful about ' manibus ' then.*

[4] *' Subdo ' (lit. ' put under ') = ' apply.'*

[5] *' Confertus ' = ' dense,' ' packed.'*

Neptune gives calm after a storm at sea.

Sic ait, et dicto citius tumida aequora placat
Collectasque fugat nubes solemque reducit.
Cymothoe[1] simul et Triton adnixus acuto
Detrudunt[2] naves scopulo ; levat ipse tridenti
Et vastas aperit Syrtes et temperat aequor
Atque rotis summas levibus perlabitur undas.
Ac veluti magno in populo cum saepe coorta est
Seditio, saevitque animis ignobile vulgus,
Iamque faces et saxa volant (furor arma ministrat),
Tum pietate gravem ac meritis si forte virum quem[3]
Conspexere, silent arrectisque auribus adstant ;
Ille regit dictis animos et pectora mulcet :
Sic cunctus pelagi cecidit fragor, aequora[4] postquam
Prospiciens genitor caeloque invectus aperto
Flectit equos curruque volans dat lora secundo.

[1] *Cymothoe was a sea nymph.*
[2] *' Thrust off.'*
[3] *See XXIII. 2.*
[4] *Object of ' prospiciens.'*

XXI

SE

1. ' *Se* ' and ' *suus*,' though not popular, are very useful words ; they refer to *the subject of the sentence* and make the meaning plain.

EXAMPLE :

' Gaius equo regnum suum tradidit.'

' Gaius handed over his kingdom to a horse.'

Even in a subordinate clause they can make the meaning clearer by looking back (as their name, ' reflexives,' suggests) to *the subject of the main verb*.

EXAMPLE :

' Civibus imperavit ut equus suus consul fieret.'

' He gave orders to the citizens that his horse should be made consul.'

In some clauses ' se ' and ' suus ' could refer to either of the two subjects :

EXAMPLE :

' Cives rogaverunt ut equus se moderaretur.'

either ' The citizens asked that the horse should rule them.'

or ' The citizens asked that the horse should control itself.'

In such cases the ' se ' usually looks back only to the subject of its own clause ; therefore, if the context allows it, the second meaning is more probable here.

2. Sometimes reflexives look back, not to the subject, but to an important word in the sentence; it seems unreasonable that they should thus break the rules, but the meaning is always plain.

EXAMPLES :

    (i) ' Desinant insidiari domi suae consuli.'
       ' Let them cease to lie in wait for the consul in *his* own home.'

    (ii) ' Sunt sua praemia laudi.'
       ' Merit has its own rewards.'

3. Notice ' *sese* ' and ' *semet* ' (strengthened forms of ' se ') and ' *inter se* ' (' *among themselves*,' ' *one another*,' or ' *mutually*').

EXAMPLE :

    ' Complecti inter se milites coeperunt.'
    ' The soldiers began to embrace one another.'

An ingenious donkey-driver.

Alexander quidem, dum oraculum consulit, monitus est ut eum, qui sibi e templo egredienti primus obviam venisset, interficeret. Itaque asinarium[1], qui forte ante alios omnes sibi occurrit, custodes suos rapere et ad mortem ducere iussit. Asinarius tamen, qui causam mortis suae minimē intellexit, custodes rogavit cur rex hominem innocentem ita iniustē occidere vellet; hi, cum inter se rem diu disputavissent, asinarium iterum ad regem ducere constituerunt. Tum ei quaerenti quid dignum tanto supplicio[2] fecisset Alexander, iussu oraculi narrato, respondit sese sic deo parere. At asinarius, ' Si ita est,' inquit, ' alius huic morti destinatus est: nam asinus, quem ante me agebam, prior tibi occurrit.' His verbis delectatus est Alexander; itaque, gavisus quod officio suo ita clementer fungi poterat, interfecit asinum, asinario pepercit.

[1] See heading.
[2] ' Supplicium ' = ' punishment ' or ' torture.'

The heroism of Regulus.

Tum Regulus dux, quem Carthaginienses ceperant, Romam missus est ut de pace cum civibus suis ageret ac permutationem[1] captivorum faceret. Sed Romam cum venisset, inductus in senatum, nihil quasi Romanus egit, dixitque se ex illo die, quo in potestatem Afrorum venisset, Romanum esse desivisse. Itaque et uxorem a complexu removit et senatui suasit ne pax cum Carthaginensibus fieret : illos enim fractos tot casibus spem nullam habere ; se tanti[2] non esse, ut tot milia captivorum propter unum se et[3] senem et paucos, qui ex Romanis capti erant, redderentur. Itaque obtinuit[4]. Nam Afros pacem petentes nemo admisit. Ipse Carthaginem rediit, et ibi omnibus suppliciis exstinctus est.

[1] ' Exchange.'

[2] See VII. 4.

[3] This ' et ' links ' unum ' and ' senem ' : the next one links ' se ' and ' paucos.'

[4] ' He had his way.'

The sights, sounds, and seasons of the countryside.

Aspice curvatos pomorum pondere[1] ramos,
  Ut sua, quod peperit[2], vix ferat arbor onus.
Aspice labentes iucundo murmure rivos :
  Aspice tondentes fertile gramen oves.
Ecce petunt rupes praeruptaque[3] saxa capellae :
  Iam referent haedis[4] ubera plena suis.
Pastor inaequali modulatur harundine carmen,
  Nec desunt comites, sedula turba, canes.
Parte sonant alia silvae mugitibus[5] altae,
  Et queritur vitulum[6] mater abesse suum.
Poma dat autumnus : formosa est messibus aestas ;
  Ver praebet flores ; igne levatur hiems.
Temporibus certis maturam rusticus uvam
  Deligit, et nudo sub pede musta[7] fluunt.

[1] ' *Pondus, -eris* ' = ' *weight.* '
[2] From ' *pario* ' = ' *I produce.* '
[3] ' *Praeruptus* ' = ' *steep.* '
[4] ' *Kids.* '
[5] ' *Mugitus* ' = ' *mooing.* '
[6] ' *Calf.* '
[7] ' *Wine.* ' *The old way of pressing grapes was to trample them
underfoot.*

QUI

Everyone knows ' qui,' the relative, meaning
' who ' or ' which ' (or, after ' idem,' ' as '): and
' qui,' the interrogative and indefinite adjective, is
dealt with in ch. XXIII. But the following two
points are not always known.

1. ' Qui ' is often used at the beginning of a
sentence in order to connect that sentence with the
one before. When used thus, parts of ' qui '
should not be translated as ' who ' or ' which,' but
as ' *he*,' ' *they*,' ' *it*,' ' *this*,' etc., according to the
context.

EXAMPLE :

> ' Quo cognito, Caesar protinus equites emisit ;
> qui cum proelium commisissent, hostes terga
> verterunt.   Quod magno auxilio nostris erat.'

> ' When he learnt of this, Caesar immediately
> sent out the cavalry : when these had joined
> battle, the enemy turned and fled.   This success
> was of great assistance to our men.'

2. ' Qui,' followed by the subjunctive, often
denotes purpose.   This construction should be carefully distinguished from the ordinary relative clause.

EXAMPLE :

> ' Legatos misit qui nuntiarent . . .'
> ' He sent envoys to report (lit. who might
> report) . . .'

[' Legatos misit qui nuntiaverunt . . .'
' He sent envoys who reported . . .']

' *Dignus qui* . . .' (' worthy to . . .'), ' *ut qui* . . .,'
' *quippe qui* . . .' (' in that he . . .,' ' because
he . . .'), ' *is qui* ' (' the kind of person who . . .'),
and ' *sunt qui* . . .' (' there are some who . . .'), are
also followed by the subjunctive.

EXAMPLES :

    (i) ' Augustus, quippe qui sit sapiens, dignus
        est qui imperet.'

     ' Augustus, in that he is wise, is worthy to
        rule.'

    (ii) ' Sunt qui putent . . .'
     ' There are some who think . . .'

Note.—The subjunctive is used whenever (as
with ' *sunt qui* . . .') the verb has an *indefinite*
force : ' qui ' will then sometimes have to be
translated as ' *whosoever*.'

The death of Atys.

Croesus, rex Lydiae, somnio nocturno[1] monitus est filium suum Atyn, iuvenem audacem, hastā vulneratum moriturum esse. Haud multo post civitas vicina[2] legatos misit, qui regem rogarent ut Atys aprum[3], qui agros vastabat, occideret; sed rex, somnio territus, filium emittere nolebat. Quo audito, Atys ad patrem suum vēnit et, ' Nonne sum dignus,' inquit, ' qui mittar ? Nam in urbe sunt qui me timidum et infirmum esse dicant.' Cum rex totum somnium aperuisset[4], respondit, ' Hoc somnium, o pater, non me terret; aper enim non is[5] est qui hastā homines vulneret.' Quibus verbis confirmatus, Croesus eum ire sivit, sed amicum fidelem, qui iuvenem custodiret, et multos servos simul emisit. Qui cum circum aprum in silvā starent, et omnes iam aprum transfigere cuperent, amicus, hastā proiectā, non aprum sed Atyn percussit; itaque filius Croesi, ut somnium praedicaverat, hastā interfectus est.

[1] *This word can be guessed from the root, from the sense, and from an English word derived from it.*

[2] ' *Vicinus, -a, -um* ' = ' *neighbouring.*'

[3] ' *Aper* ' = ' *boar.*'

[4] ' *Aperio* ' = ' *reveal.*'

[5] *Think carefully—' the kind of* person ' *will not do here.*

Varro, follower of Pompey and governor of Western Spain, finds that almost all hands are against him, and surrenders himself and his last loyal legion to Caesar.

His cognitis rebus altera ex duabus legionibus, quae vernacula[1] appellabatur, ex castris Varronis, adstante et inspectante ipso, signa sustulit[2] seque Hispalim recepit atque in foro et porticibus consedit. Quod factum cives Romani eius regionis adeo comprobaverunt, ut apud se[3] quisque militem cupidissime reciperet. Quibus rebus perterritus Varro, cum, itinere converso, se Italicam venturum esse nuntiavisset, certior ab suis factus est praeclusas esse portas. Tum vero, omni interclusus itinere, ad Caesarem legatos mittit qui de deditione loquantur; ille ad eum Sextum Caesarem mittit atque huic legionem tradi iubet.

[1] ' *Native.*'

[2] *When they marched off, legions took up the standards which they had planted in the ground when they encamped.*

[3] ' *To his own home.*'

[4] *Hispalis (the modern Seville) and Italica are towns in Spain.*

Illness in a foreign country.

Ibitis Aegaeas sine me, Messalla, per undas,
 O utinam memores ipse cohorsque mei!
Me tenet ignotis aegrum Phaeacia terris :
 Abstineas avidas, Mors, precor, atra, manus.
Abstineas, Mors atra, precor : non hic mihi mater
 Quae legat in maestos[1] ossa perusta[2] sinus,
Non soror, Assyrios cineri quae dedat odores
 Et fleat effusis ante sepulchra comis,
Delia non usquam quae, me quam[3] mitteret urbe,
 Dicitur ante omnes consuluisse deos.
Cuncta[4] dabant reditus : tamen est deterrita numquam
 Quin[5] fleret nostras respiceretque vias.

[1] *This agrees with ' sinus,' but you had better translate it by an adverb.*

[2] *You may be able to see of what verb this is a compound: or to guess the meaning from ' cineri ' in the next line.*

[3] *See XXV, Note 1.*

[4] *Understand ' omens.'*

[5] *See XXVII. 4. (i).*

XXIII

QUIS

1. '*Quis*' is used as an *interrogative pronoun*, meaning '*who*,' '*which*,' etc.: its adjective is '*qui*.'
EXAMPLE:

> '*Quid dicit?*   Quod scelus admisit?'
> '*What does he say?*   What crime has he committed?'

An *indirect question* may look very like a '*relative +*
subjunctive' construction (see ch. XXII. 2): but the form '*quis*' or '*quid*' betrays an *indirect question*, and, even where '*quis*' and '*qui*' have the same forms, common sense usually shows you what is meant, provided that you are on your guard for both possibilities.

EXAMPLES:

> (i) (Indirect question)
>   '*Rogat quid bibat.*'
>   '*He asks what he is drinking.*'
> (ii) (Relative denoting purpose)
>   '*Rogat quod bibat.*'
>   '*He asks for something to drink.*'

Note 1.   '*Nescio quis*' (lit. '*I know not who . . .*') is commonly treated as a pronoun meaning '*someone.*'
Note 2.   '*Quid . . . ?*' commonly means '*Why . . . ?*'
Note 3.   Cicero is very fond of using '*quid ?*' alone or with a particle, for rhetorical effect: sometimes this can be translated as '*What?*' but often '*Again . . .*' or '*How is this?*' is a better translation in the context.

EXAMPLES :

  (i) ' Quid deinde ? '
      ' What next ? '
  (ii) ' Quid ?   Nonne tu . . .'
      ' Again, did you not . . .'

2. ' *Quis* ' is used as an *indefinite pronoun*, meaning
' *anyone*,' etc., after ' *si*,' ' *nisi*,' ' *ne*,' and occasionally
after ' *cum* ' or ' *ubi*.' Again ' *qui* ' supplies the adjective

EXAMPLE :

  ' Si cui persuasit, gaudet.'
  ' If he persuades (lit. has persuaded) anyone, he
    is glad.'

Note. 1.   In this use the form ' *quă* ' is sometimes
found as Nom. Fem. Sing. or as Neuter Plur.

Note 2.   Other words generally used interro-
gatively have this indefinite force after " si,' e.g.
' *si quando* . . .' = ' *if ever* . . .'

3. ' *Quīs* ' is an *alternative form of* ' *quibus* ' and may
be the dative or ablative plural of ' qui ' or ' quis.'

4. Note carefully the following *compounds of* ' *quis* '
and their meanings :—

        quisnam ? = ' who, pray . . .'
        (a dramatic form of ' quis ')
        ecquis ? = ' is there anyone who . . .'
        quisque = ' each.'
        quisquam = ' anyone.'
        aliquis   = ' someone.'
        quispiam = ' anyone,' ' someone.'
        quisquis = ' whoever.'
        (quicunque)

Note. ' *Si quis* ' is sometimes used with the same
meaning as ' *quisquis*.'

The self-control of Sous.

Magnam sui famam apud Lacedaemonios reliquit Sous : dum enim hostes exercitum eius nescio quo in loco obsident nec quemquam e militibus aquam de fonte vicino ducere patiuntur, hic, indutiis[1] factis, promisit se omnes regiones quīs in eo bello potitus esset dediturum esse, dummodo omnes Lacedaemonii de fonte biberent. Tum copias suas convocatas ita adlocutus est : 'Quisnam patriae vult esse saluti[2] ? Vel quis bene de me merebitur ? Omnibus enim iam licet bibere ; at si quis occasionem bibendi praetermiserit[3] regnum meum accipiet.' Sed tam diu milites aquā caruerant ut sitim suam quisque expleverit : ergo Sous, vultu suo aquā tantum consperso[4], exercitum deduxit ; nec regiones ipsas quas ceperat restituit, quod[5] e Lacedaemoniis haud omnes bibissent.

[1] ' Indutiae ' = ' truce.'
[2] See VIII. 1. (e).
[3] ' Praetermitto ' = ' give up,' ' forgo.'
[4] See XV. 3. (i).
[5] See XXIV. 2.

It is best to be ignorant of the future.

Atque ego ne utilem quidem arbitror esse nobis futurarum rerum scientiam. Quae enim vita fuisset Priamo, si ab adulescentia scivisset quos eventus senectutis esset habiturus? Abeamus a fabulis, propiora videamus. Quid igitur? Ut omittamus superiores, Marcone Crasso putas utile fuisse tum, cum maximis opibus fortunisque florebat, scire sibi, interfecto Publio filio exercituque deleto, trans Euphratem cum ignominia et dedecore esse pereundum? An Cn. Pompeium censes tribus suis consulatibus, tribus triumphis, maximarum rerum gloria laetaturum fuisse[1], si sciret se in solitudine Aegyptiorum trucidatum iri, amisso exercitu, post mortem vero[2] ea consecutura, quae sine lacrimis non possumus dicere? Quid enim posset eis esse laetum exitus suos cogitantibus? Et si certum est quid quaque de re futurum sit, quid est quod me adiuvent haruspices[3], cum res tristissimas portendi dixerunt?

[1] *Tr.* ' . . . *would have been able to take pleasure in* . . .'

[2] ' *Vero* ' *links a second statement clause (subject* ' *ea* ') *to* '*se* . . . *trucidatum iri.*'

[3] ' *Haruspex* ' = ' *soothsayer,* ' ' *prophet.*'

A storm at sea.

Me miserum, quanti montes volvuntur aquarum!
    Iam iam tacturos sidera summa putes.
Quantae diducto subsidunt aequore valles!
    Iam iam tacturas Tartara nigra putes.
Quocunque adspicio, nihil est nisi pontus et aer;
    Fluctibus hic tumidus, nubibus ille minax[1].
Inter utrumque fremunt immani murmure venti:
    Nescit cui domino pareat unda maris.
Rector[2] in incerto est, nec quid fugiatve petatve
    Invenit.   Ambiguis ars stupet ipsa malis.
Scilicet occidimus, nec spes est ulla salutis:
    Dumque loquor, vultus obruit unda meos.

[1] *Understand ' est ' with each half of the line.*
[2] *Who is the ' rector ' of a ship ?   Think of the English ' direct.'*

XXIV

QUOD

1. ' Quod ' may be the *neuter singular of* ' *qui* ' : if you have read the last two chapters you know what that involves.

2. ' Quod ' commonly means ' *because* ' (like ' *quia* ' and ' *quoniam* '). After ' quod ' in this sense the *indicative* shows that the reason is presented as a *fact*, the *subjunctive* that it is presented as an *opinion* (tr. ' *on the grounds that* . . .').

EXAMPLES :

    (i) ' Insula capta est quod dux nimis lentum se praebuit.'
        ' The island was captured because the commander proved too slow.'

    (i) ' Ducem culpabant quod officio defuisset.'
        ' They blamed the commander on the grounds that he had failed in his duty.'

Note.—' *Eo* ' or ' *idcirco* ' or ' *propterea*,' in the main sentence, is sometimes used to strengthen ' quod ' in this sense.

3. ' Quod ' (with the indicative) may mean ' *that* . . .', ' *the fact that* . . .', ' *as for the fact that* . . .'

EXAMPLES :

> (i) ' Accidit quod multi cladem aegre ferebant.'
>> ' It happened that many people were angry about the defeat.'
>
> (ii) ' Quod ducem interfecerunt, non bene egerunt.'
>> ' They did not do well to kill the commander.'
>>
>> [lit. ' As for the fact that they killed . . ..']

4. ' Quod ' (with indicative or subjunctive) is sometimes used in a *restrictive* sense, meaning ' *as far as.*'

EXAMPLES :

> (i) ' Nemini, quod sciam, animus hac re augetur.'
>> ' As far as I know, no one is encouraged by this action.'
>
> (ii) ' Quod ad me attinet, hoc nihil proderit.'
>> ' As far as I am concerned, this will not help at all.'

Note.—See XVIII. 1. Note 1 for ' *quod si.*'

A murderer is found out.

Quot maleficia impune tulerunt[1] auctores ? Multa,
quod sciam. Sed ferunt sculptorem quendam, cui
auro opus esset, senem aliquando necavisse; et hic,
ut narrat fabula, priusquam periit haec verba aequo
animo rettulit: ' Quod me propter pecuniam
occidisti, reprehendo cupiditatem tuam. Nunc
tamen, quod ad me attinet, mori non vereor : sed tu,
qui vives, secundā fortunā nunquam utēris ; nam sol,
qui omnia aperit, hoc scelus quoque in lucem pro-
feret.' Multis post annis, cum omnia iam sibi
prosperē evenisse speraret, accidit quod forīs[2]
sculptor sedebat; tum, radio solis viso, parumper
timebat, memor verborum senis, sed mox, animo
erecto, ' O sol,' inquit, ' quid est quod facias ? Scelus
nostrum diu aperire conatus nihil efficis.' Ad-
stabat uxor : quod scelus olim admisisset cognovit :
mox caedes, sole patefacta, in ore erat omnium :
supplicium de sculptore sumpserunt[3] iudices.

[1] ' Impune fero ' = lit. ' carry off unpunished.' Put this into
English.

[2] 'Out of doors ' (sometimes = ' abroad ').

[3] Discover the literal meaning of the sentence: then express it in
good English.

Scipio restores a holy statue to Segesta.

Fuit apud Segestanos Dianae simulacrum[1] cum summa atque antiquissima praeditum religione[2] tum singulari opere artificioque perfectum. Quod, translatum Carthaginem, locum tantum hominesque mutarat[3], religionem[2] quidem pristinam conservabat; nam propter eximiam pulchritudinem etiam hostibus digna quam sanctissime colerent videbatur. Aliquot saeculis post P. Scipio Carthaginem cepit; qua in victoria convocatis Siculis omnibus, quod diutissime saepissimeque Siciliam vexatam a Carthaginiensibus esse cognorat[3], iubet omnia conquiri[4]; pollicetur sibi magnae curae fore ut omnia civitatibus, quae cuiusque fuissent[5], restituerentur. Illo tempore Segestanis maxima cum cura haec ipsa Diana, de qua dicimus, redditur.

[1] *Look at the heading.*
[2] *' Religio ' here means ' sanctity.'*
[3] *See XXVII. 1. (d).*
[4] *See XV. 3. (i).*
[5] *What do you expect this clause to mean ? Does the literal meaning of the Latin fit in with that ?*

The lover makes light of the toil of the countryside.

Rura meam, Cornute, tenent villaeque[1] puellam :
    Ferreus est, heu heu, quisquis in urbe manet.
Ipsa Venus latos iam nunc migravit in agros,
    Verbaque aratoris rustica discit Amor.
O ego, cum aspicerem dominam, quam fortiter illic
    Versarem valido pingue bidente[2] solum
Agricolaeque modo curvum sectarer aratrum,
    Dum subigunt steriles[3] arva serenda boves l
Nec quererer quod sol graciles exureret artus[4],
    Laederet et teneras pustula[5] rupta manus.
Pavit et Admeti tauros formosus Apollo[6] ;
    Nec cithara intonsae profueruntve[7] comae,
Nec potuit curas sanare salubribus herbis :
    Quidquid erat medicae vicerat artis amor.

[1] ' *Villa* ' = ' *farm.* '

[2] ' *Bidens* ' = (m.) ' *hoe* '; (*f.*) ' *sheep.* ' Which *adjective goes with it?*

[3] *Translate* ' *steriles boves* ' *as* ' *oxen.* '

[4] ' *Limbs.* '

[5] ' *Blister.* '

[6] *The story here is that Apollo worked for Admetus as a farm-labourer on account of love.*

[7] *This* ' *-ve* ' *is misplaced: it links* ' *intonsae comae* ' *to* ' *cithara.* '

XXV

QUAM

1. ' Quam ' may be simply the *accusative feminine singular of* ' *qui* ' *or* ' *quis* ' : see chs. XXII and XXIII for its possible uses in this sense.

EXAMPLE :

 ' Quam ob rem . . .' = ' Therefore . . .'

2. ' Quam ' is used *in comparisons* to mean ' *than,* ' or (usually after ' *tam* ') ' *as.* '

EXAMPLE :

 ' Puer tam vorax quam fera erat.'

 ' The boy was as greedy as an animal.'

Note.—' *Quam ut* . . .' (lit. ' than so as to . . .') should be translated by the English idiom ' *too* . . . *to* . . .'

EXAMPLE :

 ' Rationis cupidior erat quam ut caveret.'

 ' He was too fond of the practice to take pre-
 cautions.' (Lit. ' more fond than so as
 to . . .').

3. ' Quam ' is used *in questions and exclamations,* meaning ' *how.* '

EXAMPLE :

 ' Nesciebat quam dirum cibum devoraret.'

 ' He did not know how dangerous was the food
 he was swallowing.'

4. ' Quam ' is used *to strengthen superlatives* (' *as . . . as possible* ').

EXAMPLE :

> ' Medici quam celerrime sunt arcessiti.'
> ' Doctors were sent for as quickly as possible.'

Note 1. The words ' *priusquam* ' and ' *antequam* ' are sometimes split up so that ' quam ' stands alone : when you meet this put the ' prius ' or ' ante ' before the ' quam ' and translate the whole word as ' *before*.'

EXAMPLE :

> ' Prius ceteros monuit ne licia manderent quam periit.'
> ' Before he died he warned others not to chew pieces of string.'

Note 2. Learn the following compounds of 'quam' and their meanings :—

quamquam = ' although.'
quamvis = ' although,' ' however much,' ' very much.'
tamquam = ' as,' ' as if,' ' as it were.'
quamlibet = ' however much.'
quamdiu = ' as long as.'

The founding of Marseilles.

Phocaeenses, exiguitate[1] patriae suae coacti, studiosius mare quam terras exercebant. Itaque in ultimam oceani oram procedere ausi ad eam regionem quā nunc est Massilia venerunt: et, cum vidissent quam amoenus esset locus, homines emiserunt qui urbem quam celerrimē conderent. Cum ad Galliam ventum esset, Simos et Protis, duces Graecorum, regem qui illos fines tenebat adierunt: sed hic in suis negotiis magis occupatus est quam ut rem tunc ageret, nam filiam more gentis illius marito inter epulas[2] electo tradere parabat. Eos igitur ante ad hoc convivium vocavit quam negotium transigerent. Et cum omnes adessent principes earum partium, virgo ipsa introducta est; quae, cum iuberetur a patre aquam porrigere ei quem virum eligeret[3], tunc, omissis omnibus, ad Graecos conversa aquam Proti porrexit: itaque ille, ex hospite gener factus, locum condendae urbis a socero accepit. Sic Massilia condita esse dicitur.

[1] ' Exiguitas ' = ' smallness.'
[2] ' Inter epulas ' = ' at a feast.'
[3] See XXII. 2. Note.

Some witty last words.

Quam me delectat Theramenes! quam elato animo est! Etsi enim flemus cum legimus, tamen non miserabiliter vir clarus emoritur. Qui cum, coniectus in carcerem triginta iussu tyrannorum, venenum biberet, reliquum sic e poculo eiecit ut id resonaret: quo sonitu reddito, arridens, ' Propino[1],' inquit, ' hoc pulchro Critiae,' qui in eum fuerat taeterrimus[2]. Graeci enim in conviviis solent nominare cui poculum tradituri sint. Lusit vir egregius extremo spiritu cum iam praecordiis[3] conceptam mortem contineret, vereque ei cui venenum praebiberat[1] mortem eam est auguratus[4] quae brevi tempore consecuta est.

[1] ' *Drink to the health of* . . .'
[2] ' *Taeter* ' = ' *savage,*' '*cruel.*'
[3] ' *Praecordia* ' *is compounded of* ' *prae-*' *and* ' *cor.*'
[4] *What did augurs do ?*

A barbarous place of exile.

Detineo studiis animum, falloque dolores;
  Experior curis et dare verba meis.
Quid potius faciam solis desertus in oris,
  Quamve malis aliam quaerere coner opem?
Sive locum specto, locus est inamabilis et quo[1]
  Esse nihil toto tristius orbe potest:
Sive homines, vix sunt homines hoc nomine digni,
  Quamque lupi saevae plus feritatis habent:
Non metuunt leges; sed cedit viribus aequum[2];
  Victaque pugnaci iura sub ense iacent.
In paucis remanent Graiae vestigia[3] linguae:
  Haec quoque iam Getico barbara facta sono.
Unus in hoc populo nemo est qui forte Latine
  Quaelibet e medio[4] reddere verba queat.

[1] ' *Than which.*'
[2] *The neuter of the adjective here means* ' *justice.*'
[3] ' *Traces* ' (*cf. English* ' *vestiges*').
[4] ' *Medium* ' *here means* ' *the local language.*'

XXVI

QUO and EO

These two words, whether found separately or in the same sentence, have several possible meanings associated with the dative and ablative cases; once again common sense must tell you which meaning is appropriate in the passage you are considering.

1. **Quo.**

' Quo ' may :—

(i) simply be *the ablative of* ' qui ' *or* ' quis ' (cf. ' quam ' and ' quod ').

(ii) mean ' *whither* ' (cf. ' *qua* ' = ' *where*').

    EXAMPLE :

      ' Quo pergis, pulchra virgo ? '

      ' Where are you going to, pretty maid ? '

(iii) stand for ' *ut* ' (' in order that ') when *introducing a final clause that contains a comparative.*

    EXAMPLE :

      ' Librum legit quo facilius linguam Latinam intellegat.'

      ' He reads the book in order to understand Latin more easily.'

(iv) mean ' *because* ' or ' *why* ' or ' *therefore*.'

    EXAMPLE :

      ' Linguae Latinae peritus erat non quo librum legisset sed quod ingenio erat acuto.'

> ' He was clever at Latin not because he had read the book but because he was intelligent.'

Note.—' *Quōque* ' may be either *the ablative of* ' *quisque* ' or ' *quo* ' with ' *-que* ' (' and ') attached.

> ' *Quŏque* ' means ' *also.*'

2. Eo.

' Eo ' may :—

(i) simply be *the ablative of* ' *is.*'

(ii) mean ' *thither.*' In this sense it is sometimes metaphorical.

EXAMPLE :

> ' Eo res adducta est ut . . .'
> ' The matter reached such a pitch that . . .'

(iii) strengthen and point to a conjunction such as ' *ut* ' (' in order that '), ' *quia* ' (' because '), or ' *donec* ' (' until '). In this sense ' eo ' rarely needs to be translated.

EXAMPLE :

> ' Eo manebat ut videret.'
> ' He was remaining in order to see.'

3. Quo . . . eo . . .

' Quo ' and ' eo ' are commonly used *to associate two comparatives*; they are not then translated in English but the comparatives appear as ' *the more . . . the more . . .*'

EXAMPLE :

> ' Quo celerius currit, eo gravius cadit.'
> ' The more quickly he runs, the more heavily he falls.'

One reason for not marrying.

Solon, vir omnium Atheniensium sapientissimus, dum apud Thalem commoratur[1], hospitem suum rogavit quārē uxorem ducere, gignere liberos nollet. Cui Thales non statim respondit sed, quo facilius alter causam intellegeret, paullo post iussit peregrinum[2] nuntiare se Athenis nuper eo advenisse. Hic Soloni, num quid novi ibi fieret roganti, respondit ut imperatum est, ' Nihil. Sed multi eo dolebant quia iuvenis quidam, patre clarissimo natus, mortuus erat : neque aderat pater, quippe qui forīs iter tum faceret.' Tum Solon quod nomen patri esset rogavit ; sed peregrinus negavit se nominis adhuc esse memorem, quamvis omnes sapientiam illius laudavissent. Quo plura audiebat, eo vehementius Solon perturbabatur : itaque, ' Solonisne filius,' inquit, ' erat is qui periit ?' ' Solonis vero.' Tum eo doloris adductus est ut Thales, subridens, ' Sis bono animo[3],' inquit : ' nam haec non verē sunt relata. At ea quae et Solonem in tantum terrorem possunt conicere mihi persuadent ne sim paterfamilias.'

[1] ' *Commoror apud . . .*' == ' *stay with . . .*'
[2] ' *Peregrinus* ' = ' *stranger.*'
[3] *See IX. 1. (vi).*

Military manœuvres.

Caesar, postquam Pompeium ad Asparagium esse cognovit, eodem cum exercitu profectus, expugnato in itinere oppido Parthinorum, in quo Pompeius praesidium habebat, tertio die ad Pompeium pervenit iuxtaque eum castra posuit et postridie eductis omnibus copiis acie instructa decernendi[1] potestatem Pompeio fecit. Ubi illum suis locis se tenere animadvertit, reducto in castra exercitu aliud sibi consilium capiendum existimavit. Itaque postero die omnibus copiis magno circuitu difficili angustoque itinere Dyrrachium profectus est, sperans Pompeium aut Dyrrachium compelli aut ab eo intercludi posse, quod omnem commeatum totiusque belli apparatum eo contulisset.

The sentences here, as often in Latin, are long ones: you will have to break them up and use more stops in an English translation.

[1] ' Decerno ' (*lit.* ' decide ' or 'settle ') *here means* ' fight.'

A soldier of Lucullus, who has lost his wallet, shows that poverty makes the best courage.

Luculli miles collecta viatica[1] multis
Aerumnis[2], lassus dum noctu stertit[3], ad assem
Perdiderat: post hoc vehemens lupus, et sibi et hosti
Iratus pariter, ieiunis[4] dentibus acer,
Praesidium regale loco deiecit, ut aiunt,
Summe munito et multarum divite[5] rerum.
Clarus ob id factum donis ornatur honestis,
Accipit et bis dena super sestertia nummum[6].
Forte sub hoc tempus castellum evertere praetor
Nescio quod cupiens hortari coepit eundem
Verbis quae timido quoque possent addere mentem:
' I, bone, quo virtus tua te vocat, i pede fausto,
Grandia laturus meritorum praemia.   Quid stas? '
Post haec ille catus[7] quantumvis rusticus: ' Ibit,
Ibit eo, quo vis, qui zonam perdidit,' inquit.

[1] ' *Savings.* '
[2] ' *Aerumna* ' = ' *toil.* '
[3] ' *Sterto* ' = ' *snore.* '
[4] ' *Ieiunus* ' = ' *hungry.* '
[5] ' *Dives* ' + *genitive* = ' *rich in . . .* '
[6] *See XXVII. 2. (b).*
[7] ' *Canny,* ' ' *crafty.* '

ET CETERA

1. Notice some *curious alternative forms* which are puzzling if you do not know them :—

(*a*) *-īs* for *-ēs* in third declension accusative plurals (*e.g.* ' hostis ' = ' enemies ').

(*b*) *-ēre* for *-erunt* in third plural perfect indicative active (*e.g.* ' amavēre ' = ' they loved ').

(*c*) *-ere* for *-eris* in second singular future (and sometimes present) indicative passive (*e.g.* ' amabere ' = ' thou wilt be loved ').

(*d*) *The omission of* ' *v* ' (and often a vowel too) in perfect stems (*e.g.* ' amarunt ' = they loved,' ' audisse ' = ' to have heard ').

(*e*) ' *Ausim* ' for ' *ausus sim* ' (' I should dare ').

2. *Archaic forms* sometimes found in classical Latin are :—

(*a*) *-ier* for *-i* in present infinitive passive (*e.g.* ' immiscerier ' = ' to be mingled ').

(*b*) *-um* for *-orum* in genitive plurals (*e.g.* ' magnanimum ' = ' magnanimorum ').

(*c*) ' *Olli*,' etc., for ' *illi*,' etc.

(*d*) ' *Potis est* ' or ' *pote est* ' for ' *potest*.'

3. Remember the *different possible meanings of* :—
   ' num ' = ' whether ' *or* ' surely not ? '
   ' utrum ' = ' whether ' *or* ' which of two ' (masc. or neut. acc. sing.).
   [In direct questions ' utrum ' is not translated.]

' tantum ' = ' only ' *or* ' so much.'

' modo ' = ' only ' *or* ' just now ' *(or* dative
     or ablative of ' modus ').

  [' modo . . . modo . . .' = ' at one time
        . . . at another . . .'.]

' vel ' = ' or ' *or* ' even ' *or* (with super-
     latives) ' the most . . . possible.'

  [' vel . . . vel . . . ' = ' either . . . or . . . '.]

And remember that the comparative can mean
     ' *quite* . . .' or ' *too* . . .,' as well as
     ' more . . .'

4. ' *Quominus* ' (lit. ' by what the less ') and
' *quin* ' (lit. ' by which . . . not . . .') are often
met in unseens before their uses have been learnt.
It is enough to say here that common meanings of
both are :—

  (i) 'from . . . -ing.'

  EXAMPLE :

     ' Me impedit quo minus ad ludos veniam.'

     ' He stops me from going to the games.'

  (ii) ' that . . . not . . . '

  EXAMPLES :

     (i) ' Nemo erat quin fleret.'

         ' There was no one that was not weeping.'

     (ii) ' Per te stat quominus eam.'

          ' It is due to you that I am not going.'

Note 1.   Common sense will often show you that
' quin ' can be translated simply by ' that ' or ' to '
(*e.g.* ' non dubito quin . . . = ' I do not doubt
that . . .').

Note 2.   ' Quin ' introducing a question means
' why not . . . ? '

138

An ingenious cook.

Servus, qui ciconiam [1] in cenam regis parabat, crure in usum suum clam avulso[2] volucrem tantum uno crure praeditam regi apposuit; quod cum is percepisset, irā commotus servum arcessivit et mortem ei minatus est. Cui alter: ' O rex optime, vel deciperis vel hoc per iocum facis. Nemo est quin sciat huic volucri unum modo crus esse.' Tum, pollicitus se hoc probaturum[3] esse, regem ad paludem duxit; cui simul atque appropinquarunt, ciconias viderunt quae stabant, ut mos est, singulis cruribus adnixae. Servus igitur, ' Num adhuc dubitas,' inquit, ' quin rem veram narraverim ? ' Rex tamen subito clamavit: et ciconiae, binis cruribus mon-stratis, rapido volatu abiere. At servus, hac speciē minimē turbatus : ' Quin istam avem, quam tibi apposui, clamore tentasti ? Forsitan et illa crus alterum monstravisset.'

[1] ' *Ciconia* ' = ' *a stork.*'
[2] ' *Avello* ' = ' *tear off.*'
[3] ' *Probo* ' = ' *prove* ' (*sometimes* ' *inspect* ' *or* ' *approve* ').

How to make allowances.

Castigabat[1] quidam filium suum, quod paulo sumptuosius equos et canes emeret. Huic ego iuvene digresso : ' Heus tu, nunquamne fecisti quod a patre corripi[1] posset ? Fecisti, dico, non inter-dum[2] facis, quod filius tuus, si repente pater ille, tu filius, pari gravitate reprehendat[1] ? Non omnes homines aliquo errore ducuntur ? Non hic in illo sibi, in hoc alius indulget ? ' Haec tibi admonitus immodicae severitatis exemplo pro amore mutuo scripsi, ne quando tu quoque filium tuum acerbius duriusque tractares. Cogita et illum puerum esse et te fuisse atque ita hoc, quod es pater, utere, ut memineris et hominem esse te et hominis patrem. Vale.

[1] ' *Castigare,*' ' *corripere* ' *and* ' *reprehendere* ' *all mean much the same. From the sense and from English words you can guess the meaning.*

[2] ' *Interdum* ' = ' *occasionally.*' ' *Non* ' *goes closely with it.*

Pallas is borne home dead to his father Evander.

Et iam Fama volans, tanti praenuntia luctus,
Evandrum Evandrique domos et moenia complet,
Quae modo victorem Latio Pallanta ferebat.
Arcades ad portas ruere, et de more vetusto
Funereas rapuere faces.   Lucet via longo
Ordine flammarum, et late discriminat[1] agros.
Contra turba Phrygum veniens plangentia iungit
Agmina.   Quae postquam matres succedere tectis
Viderunt, maestam incendunt clamoribus urbem.
At non Evandrum potis est vis ulla tenere;
Sed venit in medios; feretro Pallanta reposto[2]
Procubuit super, atque haeret lacrimansque
                              gemensque,
Et via vix tandem voci laxata dolore est:
' Non haec, o Palla, dederas promissa parenti
Cautius ut saevo velles te credere Marti! '

[1] ' *Separates.*'   *The line of torches shows where the road runs
between fields.*

[2] ' *Feretro reposto* ' = ' *when the bier was set down.*'

NOTES

Part I

1 A. To us the sister's action seems natural, but this story, like that of Regulus (21 B), emphasises the stern ways of the Romans of old.

　　To what does a man owe his chief loyalty—to his family, to his country, or to something still wider? Consider Edith Cavell's famous words, 'I realize that patriotism is not enough.'

1 B. Caesar's first landing in Britain (55 B.C.) was strongly opposed: and his men, who had no landing-craft and no experience of 'combined operations,' had difficulty in getting ashore. Notice here the effect of a bold example and the sanctity of the 'eagle,' which was to a Roman legion what its colours are to a regiment nowadays.

1 C. There are two common ways of looking at early man: one pictures him as rough and uncivilized, the other dwells on his innocence and simple honesty. The Romans knew both views, and Tibullus (the author of this extract) writes elsewhere of man's rise from primitive savagery.

　　Does each picture contain some truth? Or were our grandfathers right in thinking that the writings of Darwin and the Book of Genesis could not both stand? Distinguish between material and moral progress.

2 A. 'By uniting we stand' is a platitude: so is its converse, 'Divide et impera.' What instances do you know of the truth of these sayings?

2 B. Should a leader wear conspicuous clothing? Over against this incident set the fate of Flaminius at Trasimene (20 B) and of Nelson at Trafalgar. You might also read 1 Kings xxii. 30–37.

2 C. These hexameters are by Virgil who perfected the metre and always used it. Notice the half-line (l. 7): of the many in the 'Aeneid,' some seem poignant, others merely unfinished.

Do you think the second line conjures up an effective picture ? Is the whole piece exciting as a description of the first sight of a promised land ?

3A. This tale is reminiscent of the ' Arabian Nights,' but comes from Herodotus, a Greek historian whose stories are so good that his truthfulness is sometimes doubted.

Attempts to propitiate the gods by sacrificing something very precious were common in antiquity and are not unknown nowadays : how far is the instinct a good one ?

3B. The wicked but witty often sound more attractive than the good but dull, especially to people who prize Sense of Humour highly.

> ' If all the good people were clever,
> And all clever people were good, . . .'

How would you finish this light poem ? Then find out how Elizabeth Wordsworth finishes it.

3C. When the ancients wanted to mark something as exceptional or to insist that their purpose would never change, they often gave a catalogue of events contrary to nature (*cf.* Isaiah xi. 6–9 ; Virgil, Eclogue IV ; Horace, Epode XVI). You may know the Elizabethan song ' Orpheus with his lute . . .,' or Burns' ' O my Luve's like a red, red rose,' or other poems which employ the same device.

4A. This is a type of bold answer, made in the martyrs' spirit of ' no compromise.' ' I had rather be a doorkeeper in the house of my God : than to dwell in the tents of ungodliness.'

4B. This ghost-story of Pliny's begins like one by Algernon Blackwood. How would you finish it ?

4C. These noble lines, put into a Roman mother's mouth by Propertius, remind one of Shakespeare's ' No longer mourn for me . . .,' or Christina Rossetti's ' When I am dead, my dearest . . .' ; but, in true Roman style, they are more practical—like the Duchess of Malfi's :

> ' I pray thee, look thou giv'st my little boy
> Some syrup for his cold, and let the girl
> Say her prayers ere she sleep.'

5A. A typical anecdote of the ' Irish ' type.

5B. This place, like the north shore of Lake Trasimene, was a natural trap : the Romans walked into it in 321 B.C., and were defeated and sent ' under the yoke ' by the Samnites.

5C. A common wish (' O for the wings of a dove ') : but Ovid, despite his genuine nostalgia, thought—like many Romans—that a poet should show himself ' learned,' and so he decks it out with appeals to mythology.   Such use of names can be majestic (as often in Milton) but is sometimes merely artificial.

6A. Dreams have always fascinated men, and a dream that came twice was, for obvious reasons, thought especially prophetic (cf. Joseph's and Pharaoh's dreams).   In late romances and in the middle ages stories of dreams were very popular.   For a recent suggestion see J. W. Dunne's ' Experiment with Time.'   Do you think events are ever revealed by dreams ?

6B. Should a captain go down with his ship ?

6C. Tibullus here revels in morbid emotion.   As love and death are the most frequent themes of poets, it is not surprising that they are often combined.

> ' What is this world ?   What asketh men to have ?
> Now with his love, now in his colde grave
> Allone, withouten any compaignye.'

7A. Both the heroes of this story were proverbial for their cunning : ' when Greeks joined Greeks, then was the tug of war! '   According to some accounts Ulysses got his own back at Troy : he forged a letter from Priam to Palamedes, and had the latter put to death for treason.

7B. Caesar's style is extraordinarily dispassionate.   Do you suppose that he had any motive for making himself out to be a plain man in his ' Commentaries ' ?

7C. The opening of this poem by Catullus is well known and has often been imitated in English, notably by Campion and Jonson. The metre (hendecasyllables) was tried by Tennyson:

> ' O you chorus of indolent reviewers,
> Irresponsible, indolent reviewers . . .'

8A. The Greek prophecies known as the Sibylline Books were consulted in Rome at times of crisis in order that the will of the gods might be learnt.

Do you think the economics of the story sound? If you had the only two existing specimens of a stamp and burnt one, would the other become twice as valuable?

8B. Do you know of any other occasions when bravery atoned for a mistake?

8C. The ancients, and the Elizabethans after them, made ideas of this sort commonplace: but even so it is a striking thought that drops of water eventually hollow out a stone. You may be able to recall some other sayings about Time, a most fertile subject.

9A. In fable the fox is almost always the wily character, but sometimes he in his turn is cheated (as in the ' Nun's Priest's Tale ' by Chaucer).

9B. This is a good example of Cicero's method of impressing a jury. Do you find it convincing, or does he ' protest too much '? And can you guess what follows?

9C. Everyone knows how, despite Laocoon's ' Timeo Danaos et dona ferentes,' the horse was taken in and ruined Troy. If you believe the legend to be founded on fact, and credit the Trojans with some common sense, you may agree with the suggestion that the ' horse ' was an abandoned siege-engine, taken as a trophy.

10A. Compare the story of Wolfe's death at the capture of Quebec.

10B. The cunning of Themistocles and the integrity of Aristides were proverbial: Plutarch tells of an Athenian who was voting for the ostracism (banishment) of Aristides because he was tired of hearing him called ' The Just.'

Is it ever justifiable to prefer expediency to honesty?
Is honesty ' the best policy '?

10C. Lucretius, afraid of death and of what the gods might do, found comfort in the materialism of Epicurus' teachings.

Notice the varied poetry at the end of this passage: mouth-filling phrases alternate with lines of extreme simplicity (8, 10,) as in Shakespeare's

> ' If thou didst ever hold me in thy heart,
> Absent thee from felicity awhile,
> And in this harsh world draw thy breath in pain,
> To tell my story.'

11A. The whole point of this story turns on whether ' Romanis ' is a dative of advantage or of disadvantage.

What effect did the capture of spoils from the East have on the Romans ?

11B. You can probably quote Macaulay's lines based on this piece. Do you think the story is true, exaggerated, or wholly mythical ?

11C. This popular legend has been the basis of several poems and operas. What happened to Orpheus afterwards ? See Milton's ' Lycidas.'

12A. To quarrel ' about an ass's shadow ' became a byword for futile quibbling, and is found even in Italian. The ass features in many Greek and Roman proverbs.

12B. Despite this fine tribute Livy blackens Hannibal's character later. He was prejudiced against an enemy commander : some modern biographers, going to the other extreme, have been over-generous to opponents.

Notice the balance and antithesis of the closing sentences, foreshadowing Tacitus and the rhetorical style of Silver Latin.

12C. Ovid, with his poet's eye, sees Troy's fall in his domestic grief and makes a romantic picture of this long farewell. What was his purpose in evoking pity like this ?

13A. According to Herodotus and Plutarch, Themistocles still only received a kind of consolation prize, for cleverness— and that from the Spartans.

13B. Often in history regular soldiers have been troubled by the tactics of light-armed guerillas.

13C. A common sentiment among poets: compare Dekker's

> ' Art thou poor, yet hast thou golden slumbers ?
> O sweet content! . . .'

Do you think happiness possible in extreme poverty ?

14A. If a prediction is ambiguous enough, it is almost sure to prove true. The Delphic oracle made use of this fact: do you know of any modern attempts to forecast the future which do the same ?

14B. To an active people, like the Greeks, old age was miserable, though where wisdom was prized the old were respected.

Compare with the end of this piece Ovid's famous words:

> ' Video meliora proboque,
> Deteriora sequor.'

14C. Tibullus lived in an age weary of war (c. 60–19 B.C.); he dreams of rural peace like Yeats in ' The Lake Isle of Innisfree.'

Notice the countryman's idea of Hades—a place with no crops.

15A. Does poetic genius really prove a man capable of managing his affairs ? You may know of some great poems written by men whom the world accounted mad.

15B. This letter, written to console Cicero for the death of his daughter, has been much admired; Sterne, who got it from Burton's ' Anatomy of Melancholy,' uses it with effect in ' Tristram Shandy.'

The thought is a poetic one: Troy and Babylon are often cited as great cities that are no more, and Shelley's ' Ozymandias' finely expresses the same idea.

15C. Roman education centred more and more on the subject chosen by Ovid's brother—rhetoric. For the last two lines cf. Pope's

> ' I lisped in numbers, for the numbers came.'

16A. The question underlying this story from Herodotus is the same as that which the book of Job treats, ' Why do righteous men suffer ? '; but the Greeks could give as a reason the caprice of a god, an answer which the Jews would not allow. For a poetic expression of the young king's bitter feelings see Matthew Arnold's ' Mycerinus.'

16B. Evacuations of this sort are recent history : in 1943 the Germans were in the same plight as Curio's men and in the same place.

16C. You may have seen the throng of Bacchus in a famous picture by Titian, or read about them in Keats' ' Song of the Indian Maid ' from ' Endymion.'

> ' Whence came ye, jolly Satyrs, whence came ye,
>   So many, and so many, and such glee ? '

17A. Relations between a general in the field and his High Command at home have always been delicate : this Hannibal, like his famous namesake, was remote from his country.

If you had been a Carthaginian senator, what would you have said at the end ?

17B. Xerxes was said to have so many men that they drank rivers dry and darkened the sun when they shot off their arrows. The oracle, which lost prestige by being ' defeatist ' during the Persian wars, was here typically ambiguous : some held that the ' wooden walls ' meant the palisade round the Acropolis.

17C. The parasite features often in Plautus and Terence, and the client was a familiar figure under the Emperors ; both types complained freely of their misfortunes. For the harshness of patrons see Johnson's Letter to Lord Chesterfield.

18A. Do bad omens affect men's morale and so cause disaster ? What is the effect of superstition nowadays ?

18B. Cicero is here following Xenophon. Do you find the arguments convincing ? You may be able to compare those of Socrates in the ' Phaedo.'

18C. ' Babes in the Wood ' stories usually have a happy ending, like this one. Children's assassins are often tender-hearted too (*see* Richard III, iv. 3).

19A. Greek philosophers held that, if anything survived death, it was only the soul; Jews and Christians spoke of the body rising again—perhaps as grain springs from seed in the ground (*see* 1 Corinthians xv).   Does it matter what happens to the body after death ?   Why ?

19B. This is by Sallust. Ancient historians liked to introduce speeches (especially before a battle), and, if they did not know what was actually said, they sometimes supplied words suitable for the occasion.

Do you know any modern instances of a speech (or message) to troops before a battle ?

19C. Virgil's Eclogues (modelled on the Idylls of Theocritus) influenced many later writers of pastoral poetry; the cult became very artificial in Europe between the sixteenth and eighteenth centuries.

The ancients generally admired quiet, cultivated landscapes : the taste for remote splendour came in with the Romantic Revival.

20A. This enchanting incident took place during Tiberius' reign, according to Plutarch : it has sometimes been given a Christian interpretation.

20B. Rashness, disregard for omens, and reforming zeal, all told against Flaminius in the eyes of Livy, who pays tribute to his courage but treats Paullus, who died at Cannae (*see* 6B), with more respect.

20C. The scene is reminiscent of baroque sculpture and painted ceilings.

Notice here how a simile can, by reference to a familiar happening, make vivid a picture which is to be imagined.

21A. The donkey-driver's excuse depends on treating an animal as equivalent to a human being.   Pythagoras, two centuries before Alexander, had taught that souls could ' migrate ' from a man to an animal (*see* Twelfth Night, iv. 2. 56–66).

21B. Regulus was the sort of man Rome bred in the early days ; but by the time Eutropius wrote this account luxury had almost destroyed the Empire. You may know Horace's version of the story (Odes III. 5). with its wonderfully quiet close.

21C. Ovid paints this pleasing, but rather conventional, picture of the country, when recommending it as a distraction for the lovesick.

Do you consider Ovid a great poet or merely a facile one ?

22A. Another good story from Herodotus. You will find a poem based on it in the Collected Poems of A. E. Housman (Additional Poems, No. 1).

22B. Varro, with his indecision and helplessness, cuts a poor figure as a soldier in the Civil War, but he was a man of great learning who wrote on such diverse subjects as farming and Latin grammar.

22C. The attentions of kinsmen after death meant much to the ancients. Notice here, and elsewhere, that elegiacs were a metre for personal poetry rather than for epic or satire.

23A. Does the argument of Sous seem to you a quibble ?

23B. It was certainly well for Cicero that he did not know his end. Most men who, in history or fiction, have had their deaths foretold have, like Macbeth and Henry IV, not understood the prophecy till its fulfilment was upon them.

Would you welcome an exact prediction of your future, knowing that you could not alter it ?

23C. The ancients were naturally wary of the sea : they avoided sailing in winter and hugged the coast as far as possible.

Compare with this account Psalm cvii. 23–30.

24A. There is a kind of poetic justice here, in that the act of boasting brings about the sculptor's downfall : in tragedy this was known as ' peripeteia.'

Do you see any improbability in the story ?

24B. Compare 9B.

Should a work of art be equally sacred to people of different religious beliefs ? Or is it then an idol ?

24C. Tibullus knew that country life was hard; many poets write only of its joys, as Marlowe does deliberately in ' Come live with me and be my love . . .'

25A. This Hollywood story reminds one that men have always tended, in their legends, to give romantic reasons for great events. Serious historians prefer serious causes : Thucydides, for instance, suggests that the Trojan war was fought for reasons of trade, not for Helen. But remember on the other side Pascal's saying : ' If Cleopatra's nose had been shorter, the whole history of the world would have been different.'

25B. There is reference here to the game of ' cottabos,' which was played at Athenian drinking-parties.

Do you know of other men who jested as they were dying ?

25C. ' My mind to me a kingdom is.' What great writers have worked, like Ovid, in bleak surroundings, exiled or in prison ?

26A. Is it reasonable to reject something pleasant because the fear of losing it would be too painful ? Such a feeling was at the bottom of the Epicurean ideal—an untroubled life—and has prompted lines like :

> ' Love thy country, wish it well,
> Not with too intense a care ;
> 'Tis enough that, when it fell,
> Thou its ruin didst not share.'

26B. Speed, surprise, and an eye to the enemy's supply problem, were then, as now, vital in warfare.

26C. The mild cynicism is typical of Horace, who prided himself on being a man of the world. But the wonder is that mercenaries, who were commonly used in ancient warfare, ever ' saved the sum of things for pay.'

27A. Boccaccio tells this delightful story, which almost certainly comes from an older source.

27B. This letter of Pliny's gives us the ancient equivalent of the ' heavy father ' and his advanced friend.

Comic writers, from Aristophanes (in the ' Clouds ')
to Anstey (in ' Vice Versa '), have often exploited the
idea of father and son having their positions reversed.

27C. An account of such an event as this (like Tennyson's
' Home they brought her warrior dead ') is almost sure
to be moving; but the effects can easily become cheap
or emotional. Note how restrained are the words
Virgil gives to Evander; they are a fine example of the
strength of the so-called ' classical ' style.